*Self-Love
and
Effective
Communication*

Self-Love and Effective Communication

Practical Advice for
Finding Your Voice to Speak Your Truth

Ryan Potter

Copyright
© 2024 by Ryan Potter.

All rights reserved. No part of this publication may be replicated, shared, or transmitted by any method, including but not limited to photocopying, recording, or other forms, without receiving written permission from the author, except for brief quotations embodied in book reviews and specific other noncommercial purposes permitted by copyright law.

Ryan Potter has no responsibility for the persistence or accuracy of URLs for external or third-party internet Websites referred to in this publication and does not guarantee that any content on such Websites is, or will remain accurate or appropriate.

ISBN-13: 979-8-9916868-9-1

First Published by Ryan Potter 2024

First Printing Edition 2024 in the United States

Self-Love and Effective Communication

Self-Love Book Publishing

Learning to Love Yourself Book

www.bodysmirks.com

Self-Love Matters

Self-neglect is the leading cause of stress.

Experience the new you!

If not now, when?

Contents

Self-Love and Effective Communication

Copyright

Contents

Introducing Self-Love and Effective Communication 1

What Is Self-Communication? 2

The Importance of Self-Communication 3

Types of Self-Communication 5

The Dangers of Negative Self-Communication 6

Emotional Self-Invalidation 7

Poor Communication Habits 8

The Potential of Positive Self-Communication 10

The Influence of Motivation 12

Forms of Communication Skills 14

Self-Development in Communication 16

Key Self-Communication Skills 17

Improving Self-Communication Skills 19

Comprehending Analytical Communication 21

Critical Thinking 23

Intuitive Reasoning 24

Logical Reasoning 26

Bias Versus Distortion 29

Grasping Cognitive Bias 30

Sensing Cognitive Distortions 34

Asking Intentional Questions 38

- Self-Expression ... 41
- Efficient Communication ... 42
- Boosting Confidence ... 44
- Expanding Imaginative Skills ... 45
- Black-and-White Thinking ... 47
- Overgeneralization ... 49
- Labeling ... 51
- Catastrophizing ... 54
- Magnification ... 56
- Minimization ... 58
- Discounting the Positive ... 60
- Mental Filtering ... 62
- Emotional Reasoning ... 64
- Should, Ought, Must Statements ... 66
- Comparison ... 68
- Personalization ... 70
- Blaming ... 72
- Jumping to Conclusions ... 75
- Mind Reading ... 77
- Fortune Telling ... 80
- Always Being Right ... 82
- The Truth Behind Illusions ... 86
- Acknowledging Denial ... 88
- Addressing Anger ... 91
- Unsettled Bargaining ... 95
- Expressing Sadness ... 97
- The Science of Tears: *More Than Just Emotion* ... 100
- The Myth of Perfection ... 102
- Reaching Acceptance ... 104
- The Reality of Facing Problems ... 105
- Common Sense: *A Worldwide Perspective* ... 106
- Venting Versus Self-Expression ... 108
- Recognizing Triggers ... 111
- Signs of Insecurity ... 115

Realizing Projection 118

Aggressive Communication 120

Setting Limits 122

Personal Boundaries 124

Rigid Boundaries 126

Diffuse Boundaries 130

How to Say No 132

When to Walk Away 134

Responding To Abuse 136

Leniency Towards Mistakes 139

Moving Forward with Forgiveness 140

Loving Deeply 142

Self-Neglect 144

Smart Goals 145

Fundamental Life Skills 147

Emotional Intelligence 149

Time Management 152

Financial Literacy 155

Resilience 159

Adaptability 161

Enacting Self-Love 164

Feel, Felt, Found 167

Embracing Healthy Discernment 169

Remaining Objective 171

The Law of Averages 173

The Influence of Greed 175

Urgent Communication 177

Impacting Indifference 179

Cognitive Reframing 181

The ABCs of Constructive Communication 183

Mismanaged Abilities 185

Practicing Mental Health 188

The Control Factor 191

Embracing Limits 193

Accountability 195

Mastering Inner Dialogue Skills 197

More To Come...

About The Author

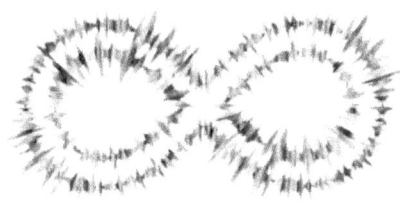

Introducing Self-Love and Effective Communication

Imagine feeling overburdened by the demands of life. Instead of overworking yourself, you exercise self-love by engaging in enjoyable activities. After experiencing relief from this break, you take a deep breath. Then, you remind yourself of all the progress you have made in the area you have been feeling overwhelmed with. To increase motivation further, you tell yourself, "I'll keep doing the best that I can."

Practicing self-care enables you to manage your well-being as well as strengthen your relationship with yourself. It also promotes personal development and inspires you to achieve your goals.

Adequate skills are necessary in all facets of life since interacting with other people is inevitable. We talk to friends, family members, teachers, coworkers, and strangers. When this happens, speaking clearly, listening intently, and demonstrating compassion are indispensable qualities.

Throughout life, we are taught to think about how we mingle with the individuals around us. We sometimes forget how crucial it is to communicate with ourselves appropriately.

Expression is a natural part of human behavior that shapes our thoughts, feelings, and actions daily. We frequently go through this experience without even noticing it. Knowing that everyone shares this trait can help us feel more connected and understood in our everyday lives.

The capability to convey ourselves clearly and confidently is an invaluable part of effective communication. Quality self-reflection is critical to our mental health and stimulates personal growth.

Self-talk can take many forms. Harnessing the power of practical skills fuels our productivity and inspires us to strive for more.

The next time you consciously have a discussion with yourself, acknowledge that it's a common and influential part of humanity. In this book, we will delve deeper into several pertinent skills, why they are worthwhile, and how you can improve them in various situations in your life.

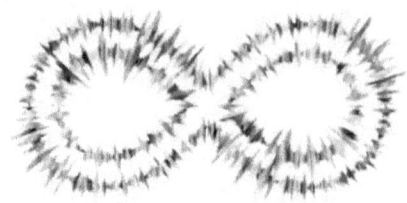

What Is Self-Communication?

Since the dawn of humanity, self-communication has been an integral part of our behavior. It's a continuous, automatic process that occurs consciously and unconsciously throughout the day. Early forms of intrapersonal communication were usually linked to religious or spiritual practices, where individuals engaged in internal dialogue to connect with higher powers or seek guidance from within.

Have you ever noticed the voice in your head that comments on everything you do? That's your internal dialogue. We all engage in conversations with ourselves, often without even realizing it. We convey messages to ourselves both mentally and verbally.

This potent mechanism can tremendously impact how you perceive yourself. It involves our inner voice, our thoughts, and how we process our experiences. It also consists of the way we interpret and respond to those messages. Understanding this can lead to greater awareness and introspection.

Self-communication can manifest in various forms, including affirmations, personal reflection, criticism, problem-solving, or simply narrating your daily experiences in your mind. We often explore concerns in our minds, weighing different options and potential outcomes. These discussions can be positive, negative, or neutral, each having a unique impact on our perceptions.

Acquiring knowledge in this area can help us understand our thought processes. As a result, we will gain more enlightenment and inspiration to make better decisions.

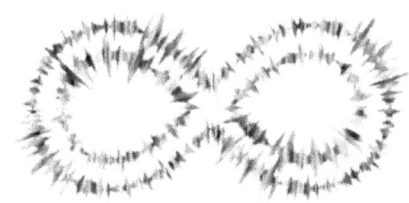

The Importance of Self-Communication

Day-to-day self-communication formulates our perceptions, thoughts, emotions, beliefs, values, and interpretations of events. Several factors, such as past experiences and external influences, affect this internal dialogue. It can impact the attitudes we hold about ourselves as well as the behaviors we display in the world around us.

Psychologists like Jean Piaget and Lev Vygotsky have shown how our inner dialogue shapes cognitive development and problem-solving skills. In 1936, Piaget's stages of cognitive development underscored how our self-talk evolves as we gain a deeper comprehension of ourselves and the world around us. Similarly, Vygotsky's approach to the zone of proximal development, in 1962, highlighted the importance of self-talk in fostering a growth mindset.

When practiced with intention and awareness, intrapersonal communication is a robust personal growth and development tool. It influences our emotions, actions, relationships, performance, and mental health. Honing our skills helps us voice our thoughts, feelings, and needs in a productive and positive manner, paving the way for a more fulfilling and balanced life.

Furthermore, internal dialogue plays a significant role in critical thinking and decision-making. When we engage in reflection, we can analyze situations from various angles, weigh the pros and cons, and make informed choices.

A work-related scenario involving a challenging project might consist of perceiving our feelings, expressing our perspective to our team, and finding a solution. This process encourages us to question our assumptions, biases, and beliefs, cultivating a growth mindset toward new ideas.

Effective skills equip us with the ability to implement innovative solutions and adapt to dynamic situations confidently. Consciously nurturing a more positive and compassionate inner voice enhances our overall well-being.

Benefits:

- **Confidence:** Good practices make you feel more confident in yourself and your abilities. This confidence helps you get out of your comfort zone, take on challenges, try new things, and overcome obstacles.
- **Emotional Well-Being:** Healthy communication is a potent tool for managing stress, anxiety, and negative emotions. It allows us to acknowledge our feelings, understand their source, and reassure ourselves, fostering resilience. This process enables us to experience our feelings and develop a positive mindset, making us feel more prepared and capable of facing challenges.

  Moreover, we can effectively convey our needs, concerns, and boundaries. When we practice compassion with ourselves, we can reduce feelings of anxiety, anger, or frustration.

  In a work setting, productive conversation may involve setting clear expectations, providing constructive feedback, and managing stress. It might include recognizing our feelings, expressing our perspectives, and finding a solution when we're in a conflict.
- **Relationships:** Strong intrapersonal communication skills empower us to develop understanding and empathy for ourselves. Knowing ourselves helps us empathize with others better. This sense of compassion nurtures mutual respect, making us feel more connected in our relationships.
- **Goal Achievement:** Enhancing your ability to set, pursue, and achieve meaningful goals is one vital area where these skills are helpful. Setting a goal might involve clarifying your objective, identifying your motivations, and planning your steps.

  When we communicate effectively with ourselves, we can clearly define our objectives, create actionable plans, and stay motivated throughout the process. This motivation and determination can be a game-changer in achieving your ambitions.

Engaging in positive affirmations is a powerful tool for boosting confidence, overcoming doubt, and modifying negative thinking patterns that may hinder our progress. Aligning our thoughts, beliefs, and actions with practical tools helps us stay focused, organized, and resilient in facing challenges. As a result, we can remain persistent while accomplishing our aspirations.

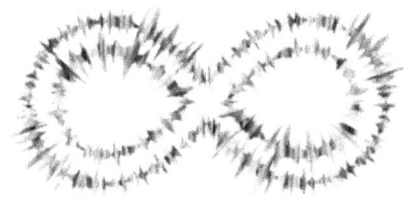

Types of Self-Communication

Philosophers in the early 4th century BCE, such as Socrates and Plato, emphasized the value of self-reflection and introspection. This acknowledgment laid the groundwork for the development of various types of self-communication.

In the modern era, psychologists, psychiatrists, and researchers have contributed significantly to studying and understanding the many forms of self-communication. Comprehending the distinct characteristics of communication with oneself can help people become more aware and improve their mental health.

Communication Styles:
1. **Positive self-talk** offers hopeful messages that are supportive and nurturing. Someone might focus on their strengths, accomplishments, and potential. We can accomplish our ambitions because the reward center in our brains is triggered in a beneficial way.
2. **Negative self-talk** is a destructive communication style. We may focus on our weaknesses, failures, and limitations. Constantly berating oneself may lead to discouragement and a willingness to give up when things get tough.
3. **Instructional self-talk** gives guidance, direction, or encouragement. It can empower us to complete tasks more efficiently, solve problems, and regulate our behaviors.
4. **Motivational self-talk** inspires us to take action and persist through difficulties. It can enhance our determination, resilience, and drive towards achieving our goals.
5. **Coping self-talk** is valuable for managing stress, emotions, and demanding situations.

Take a moment to consider your self-communication habits. Have you observed any patterns? Are there any changes you would like to make? Commit to making beneficial adjustments in your self-communication, and your mental health will improve.

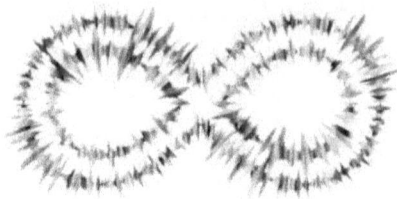

The Dangers of Negative Self-Communication

Negative self-communication can have significant consequences on our overall well-being. These beliefs stem from various sources, such as past experiences, societal pressures, or unrealistic expectations. Let's evaluate the dangers of destructive communication.

Impact:
- **Mental Health:** Individuals may struggle while dealing with everyday stressors.
- **Self-Esteem:** When people repeatedly tell themselves damaging messages, they can hinder their confidence and ability to take on new challenges.
- **Relationship with Others:** Our inner dialogue frequently influences how we interact with the world. Individuals may unknowingly project their insecurities onto friends, family members, and peers. As a result, misunderstandings, conflicts, and feelings of isolation may arise.
- **Performance:** People may be less likely to apply effort, participate in discussions, or seek help when needed, which can affect their overall success.

Becoming cognizant of these patterns allows us to recognize when we are participating in self-sabotage. Thankfully, there are strategies for combating negative self-talk.

Emotional Self-Invalidation

Many people experience emotional self-invalidation but might not fully comprehend it. It entails suppressing, ignoring, or dismissing our thoughts or feelings. When we invalidate ourselves, we tell ourselves that our feelings are not necessary or valid. As a result, our mental and emotional health may deteriorate.

For instance, if we experience sadness but convince ourselves there is no reason to be unhappy. Feelings of guilt, shame, and low self-esteem may arise because of disregarding our emotions.

In another example, assume we are apprehensive about something but convince ourselves that it isn't a huge deal. Negating our feelings can cause internalized anxiety.

Avoidance of our emotions happens when we deny our emotions instead of recognizing and processing them. Bypassing our feelings might lead to difficulties in dealing with stress.

We reject a core part of ourselves when we consistently dismiss our feelings. This can cause distress, relationship problems, and challenges with self-expression. Recognizing these side effects can encourage us to improve our validation techniques.

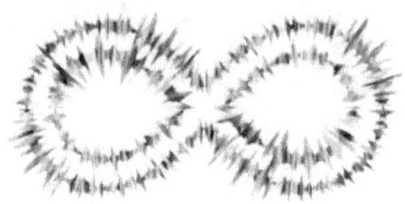

Poor Communication Habits

Poor communication refers to the difficulty of conveying thoughts, feelings, or ideas to oneself or others. Individuals with ineffective communication may struggle in many areas of life. When we do not communicate with ourselves effectively, our thoughts, feelings, and behaviors have negative repercussions. Over time, constantly criticizing ourselves, dwelling on our flaws, and questioning our abilities can make it increasingly difficult to overcome obstacles.

For example, someone may continuously persuade themselves that they are not good enough, smart enough, or deserving of success. They may start to believe it and may not even attempt to reach their full potential. This self-sabotage loop exacerbates worry and despair.

Unpleasant, unrealistic, or harmful messages create feelings of inadequacy and frustration. They disrupt relationships, impair performance, and dampen happiness.

Individuals who struggle with poor self-communication may project unresolved concerns onto those around them. This behavior could be due to low self-esteem, past experiences, or even external influences.

These detrimental habits cause unnecessary stress by preventing us from viewing things objectively. It is imperative to detect and address ineffective communication with oneself.

Impact:
1. **Lack of Self-Awareness:** Individuals out of touch with their emotions, thoughts, and behaviors may find confronting their problems internally and externally difficult. This can result in misunderstandings, misinterpretations, and an inability to resolve conflicts.
2. **Negative Self-Talk:** This damaging mental conversation can lead to feelings of unworthiness. Negative inner dialogue can impact how a person views themselves or their abilities, which influences their behavior and decision-making.

3. **Avoidance of Emotions:** When individuals suppress or ignore their feelings, they fail to acknowledge and process them effectively. Unresolved emotions might manifest as outward behaviors such as anger, irritation, or blame towards others.
4. **Lack of Assertiveness:** Individuals may have difficulty expressing themselves authentically. This can result in passive-aggressive conduct, bottling up emotions, or indirect communication methods. Preventing genuine self-expression leads to conflicts in personal and professional relationships.
5. **Unhealthy Coping Mechanisms:** Substance abuse, overeating, or excessive screen time add to the projection of unresolved concerns. These behaviors detract from addressing underlying problems and can exacerbate feelings of guilt, shame, and alienation.
6. **Blaming Others:** People may project their insecurities onto others instead of accepting responsibility for their actions. This externalization of difficulties can strain relationships and impede personal development.
7. **Comparison and Perfectionism:** When people set unrealistic standards for themselves based on external benchmarks, they may experience feelings of jealousy and self-doubt.

People who fail to communicate appropriately with themselves may find it challenging to participate in discussions, collaborate with teams, or seek clarification from others. Difficulties expressing emotions or seeking support can worsen feelings of loneliness, alienation, and worry.

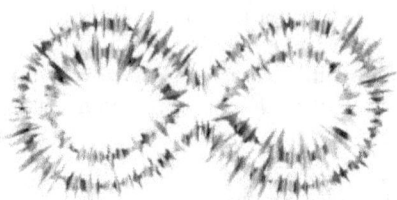

The Potential of Positive Self-Communication

Positive self-communication, also known as positive self-talk, is vital in forming our thoughts, feelings, and actions. It encompasses the messages we supply to ourselves, influencing our self-esteem, confidence, and overall well-being. Harnessing the potential of positive self-communication can provide various perks in several areas of our lives.

Positive self-communication employs constructive words and thoughts when talking to oneself. It necessitates a deliberate effort to replace negative beliefs with uplifting statements. For example, instead of saying, "I can't do this," positive language with oneself consists of reframing it into, "I will give it my best shot and learn from the experience." This transformation in our internal conversation inspires us to strive for personal excellence.

Impact:
- **Self-Esteem:** When we encourage ourselves, we boost our belief in our abilities. Acknowledging our strengths while concentrating on our progress enables us to establish a healthier self-image.
- **Confidence and Resilience:** Positive affirmation challenges our fear of failure. When we replace self-doubt with confirmations of our talents, we bolster our willingness to take on new opportunities. This allows us to bounce back from setbacks while pursuing our goals.
- **Problem-Solving Skills:** Approaching problems with a constructive mindset permits us to be more adept at navigating hardships successfully. It encourages us to learn from our mistakes rather than being discouraged by them.
- **Mental Health and Well-Being:** Practicing kindness toward ourselves significantly reduces stress levels. Building a more optimistic outlook promotes gratitude, leading to a sense of tranquility.

- **Positive Relationships:** When we treat ourselves respectfully, we are better equipped to extend compassion to those around us. This fosters a secure self-image that enhances our communication, understanding, and connection with others on a deeper level.

Positive self-communication has the capacity to shape our cognitive processing, emotions, and behaviors profoundly. Embracing self-validation gives us robust abilities as well as improves our happiness. Empower yourself with motivation while persevering through life's tests.

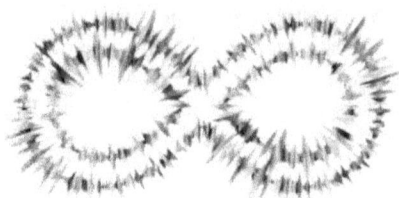

The Influence of Motivation

Motivation compels us to take action, pursue our aspirations, and overcome challenges. It's a potent influence on our attitudes, behaviors, and accomplishments. Understanding its impact can help us harness the power to achieve greater success in various aspects of our lives.

At its core, motivation urges us to act in a certain way. It pushes us to set goals, strive to reach them, and persist through obstacles. Inspiration can come from diverse sources like personal ambitions, external rewards, or persuasion from others. Our determination lies at the heart of our actions.

Two main types:
1. **Intrinsic Motivation:** Harry Harlow and Edward Deci, two renowned psychologists, were the first to identify this concept. It comes from within oneself and is directed by personal curiosity or a sense of purpose. For example, an individual who enjoys reading is intrinsically motivated to explore new books.
2. **Extrinsic Motivation:** In the 1970s, psychologists Edward Deci and Richard Ryan pioneered extensive research on this notion. It is dependent on external factors such as rewards or praise from others. For example, an athlete who trains hard to win a trophy is extrinsically motivated by the yearning for external validation.

Impact:
- In the academic realm, driven individuals are more likely to establish ambitions, maintain focus on their studies, and prevail through difficulties. Their enthusiasm for learning encourages them to seek out new knowledge, engage actively in class discussions, and work toward completing their pursuits.
- In the workplace, spirited employees aim to perform well, take on new opportunities, and contribute to the success of their organization. They exhibit high levels of productivity, creativity, and job satisfaction, leading to increased efficiency. Those who show initiative may often seek moments for growth by continuously working to improve their skills and performance.

While motivation is useful, it is not always constant. External circumstances, such as setbacks, criticism, or lack of support, can impede progress toward our objectives. Focusing on personal fulfillment is essential for sustainability. Setting attainable goals, celebrating small victories, and seeking support can help reignite us during undesirable times.

Our mindset substantially shapes our energy. It encompasses discernment of our abilities. A growth mentality is characterized by the belief that skills can progress through effort and perseverance. Embracing a healthy mental state will aid you in viewing hurdles as learning experiences, enduring setbacks, and pursuing dreams.

Motivation is a driving force that empowers us to go after our goals, overcome misfortunes, and achieve success. Understanding its distinct components propels us toward more joy. Welcoming this guiding authority inspires us to level up in life while we work on unlocking our full potential.

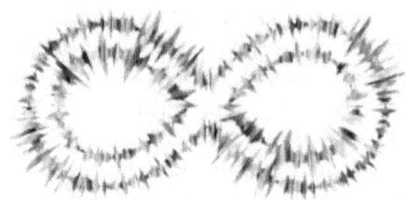

Forms of Communication Skills

Competent communication skills are necessary for success in all areas of life. Clear, constructive communication can enhance your motivation, focus, and perseverance in achieving your personal and professional goals.

Types:
- **Active listening** was popularized by a prominent humanistic psychologist named Carl Rogers in 1957. We focus on how we speak to ourselves, both mentally and verbally. We also seek to comprehend the feelings and intentions behind those messages.
- **Self-reflection** involves consciously examining your thoughts, feelings, values, beliefs, and behaviors objectively to gain insight into yourself. In 1910, Psychologist John Dewey advocated for reflective thinking as a way to enhance personal growth and learning. You'll be able to fathom your strengths and weaknesses, identify areas for personal progress, communicate more authentically, perceive the impact of your words, and make informed choices that agree with your authentic self.
- **Self-regulation** refers to the ability to manage one's thoughts, emotions, and behaviors constructively. Psychologist Walter Mischel's research on self-control and delayed gratification between 1967 and 1973 shed light on the importance of self-regulation in accomplishing long-term goals. It enables individuals to enhance their decision-making abilities, cope with stress, and maintain emotional balance.
- **Assertiveness** means expressing your thoughts, feelings, and needs clearly and respectfully. It includes advocating for what is important to you while considering your rights and feelings. Psychologists Albert Ellis and Aaron Beck promoted assertiveness training in the 1950s as a way to improve communication and self-confidence.

- **Emotional intelligence** can be described as the ability to recognize, understand, and articulate one's emotions and needs in a healthy way. In 1995, Psychologist Daniel Goleman popularized the theory of emotional intelligence and its influence on personal and professional success. We need to recognize what we require to feel fulfilled and communicate those needs clearly with ourselves and others.
- **Verbal communication** consists of speaking and using words to convey messages. Linguist Noam Chomsky's theories on language acquisition and communication in the 1950s have influenced our understanding of verbal communication skills.
- **Nonverbal communication**, such as body language, facial expressions, gestures, proximity, tone of voice, touch, and appearance, conveys messages without words. Psychologist Paul Ekman's research on facial expressions and emotions in the late 1960s and early 1970s has contributed to our knowledge of nonverbal communication cues. Adequate nonverbal communication complements verbal messages and helps to strengthen the overall impact of self-expression.
- **Written communication** transmits messages through written words, such as emails, essays, letters, and reports. Writing theorist George Hillocks emphasized the importance of clear and coherent writing for effective communication in 1984.
- **Conflict resolution** involves actively listening to ourselves, empathizing with our perspectives objectively, and working toward results-oriented solutions. Mediator William Ury's work on negotiation and conflict resolution strategies in 1981 has been instrumental in promoting peaceful resolutions in various settings. Practicing conflict resolution techniques yields positive results.

Practical skills are the core of obtaining a more balanced and fulfilling life. Developing these skills will allow you to share your unique perspectives with the world as well as achieve your personal and professional goals.

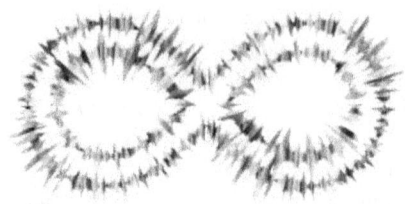

Self-Development in Communication

Self-development indicates the growth process of improving oneself mentally, emotionally, and physically. It involves setting goals, acquiring new skills, and striving toward becoming the best version of oneself. It's a lifelong journey that requires self-awareness, motivation, and perseverance.

Engaging in self-development can take many forms. Obtaining adequate skills is a valuable asset that can benefit all aspects of your life. For instance, when you're feeling stressed, being mindful of your internal thoughts or feelings allows you to analyze where your stress is coming from so that you can alleviate it.

This gateway enables you to maximize your talents. Challenging yourself to grow and improve empowers you to achieve personal fulfillment and satisfaction. Maintaining positive and empowering self-talk permits you to overcome self-doubt, fear of failure, and other barriers to success. As you witness your progress, you'll boost your self-esteem and confidence.

In today's fast-paced world, continuous learning is fundamental to staying relevant and competitive. Investing in yourself helps you increase your resilience and adaptability, making it easier to maneuver through life's ups and downs.

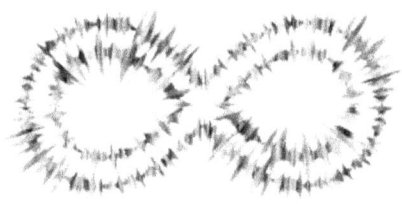

Key Self-Communication Skills

Becoming conscious of our internal dialogue is the first step towards developing our self-communication abilities. Sufficient skills allow us to understand ourselves better, boost our self-esteem, and manage our emotions successfully. Courteous communication involves being aware of how we speak to ourselves.

Mindfulness is rooted in ancient Eastern traditions like Buddhism and Hinduism. This practice consists of being completely cognizant of our thoughts or feelings. It can significantly improve self-communication.

Techniques such as meditation and journaling enable us to observe our thoughts and build a more merciful inner dialogue. Practicing an open mind allows us to observe our thoughts and feelings without becoming consumed by negativity. This emotional regulation method can help us to feel better.

Being attentive to our thoughts and feelings is paramount. It assists us in identifying patterns of thinking that may be preventing peace. Being mindful of our self-talk permits us to observe it more objectively so that we can choose to respond with loving kindness and acceptance.

Self-compassion is the discipline of extending forgiveness to ourselves. It's about acknowledging our struggles and reassuring ourselves that it's okay to make mistakes. After conducting extensive analysis on this topic, Dr. Kristin Neff advocated for it in 2003. According to research, practicing compassion is linked to improved mental health, greater emotional stability, and overall well-being.

When we practice self-respect, we pay attention to our internal dialogue while striving to be constructive and supportive. As a result, we experience enhanced emotional intelligence and a deeper connection with ourselves.

Treating oneself patiently during challenging situations can counteract negative self-talk and establish a healthier self-image. Instead of being hard on ourselves, we can practice treating ourselves with the same mercy and empathy that we would offer to a friend in need.

Empathetic self-communication is a potent personal growth tool that can help us build resilience and navigate challenges, leading to greater self-worth. It is a fundamental premise of Nonviolent Communication (NVC) formulated by Dr. Marshall Rosenberg in the 1960s and 1970s.

We become attuned to our needs, allowing us to respond with care and compassion. Self-awareness is essential for our mental health and serves as the foundation for emotional intelligence.

Engaging in compassionate self-communication provides numerous benefits. It can help us cope with stress, manage difficult emotions, and overcome setbacks. Reassuring ourselves creates a more positive and supportive internal dialogue that promotes our personal growth. We can nurture our self-esteem and build a more sympathetic connection with ourselves.

Moreover, empathetic self-communication has a profound impact on our relationships with others. When we are kind and understanding towards ourselves, we are better equipped to offer the same empathy to those around us. This generates a positive feedback loop of compassion that strengthens our social bonds.

Developing critical self-communication skills such as mindfulness, self-compassion, and empathetic self-communication can enhance one's awareness as well as boost self-esteem. Cognizance subsequently creates the path for constructive self-communication, allowing people to overcome obstacles, make informed decisions, and sustain healthy interactions. The voyage for self-improvement is rewarding and encourages us to continue strengthening these skills.

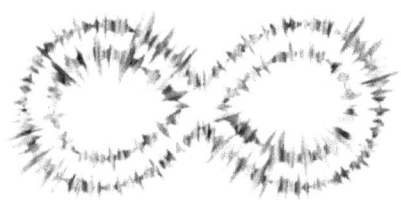

Improving Self-Communication Skills

Self-communication skills encompass a range of abilities that allow individuals to understand, manage, and express their thoughts, feelings, and beliefs effectively. These skills are the foundation of regulating oneself. Developing healthy habits takes practice and patience. This journey requires us to be gentle with ourselves. Changing ingrained thoughts can take time.

Tips:
1. **Goals:** Make sure to set realistic expectations. Recognize your strengths and weaknesses.
2. **Self-Awareness:** Pay attention to your thoughts, emotions, and behaviors. Be honest with yourself about what you are experiencing. Are you being kind, compassionate, and supportive, or are you being critical and demeaning?
3. **Journaling:** Process your inner dialogue. Express yourself freely while you reflect on your experiences. You may uncover underlying limiting beliefs that may be holding you back.
4. **Self-Validation:** Acknowledge your emotions as valid and worthy of compassion. Treat yourself with the same kindness and respect you would offer to other people you care about. Embrace yourself completely.
5. **Affirmations:** Reinforce conviction in your abilities through positive statements. Regularly affirm your qualities, strengths, values, and past successes. Daily affirmations can boost confidence, self-esteem, resilience, and persistence.
6. **Gratitude:** Recognize your talents. Acknowledge and celebrate your accomplishments, no matter how small. You can enhance your determination to progress towards your goals.
7. **Support and Feedback:** Surround yourself with positivity, such as inspirational books and quotes. Reach out for help when needed. Seek guidance from a qualified professional to improve your self-communication skills.

A qualified individual ensures that you receive reliable advice. Avoid unqualified individuals because they may not have the skills necessary to help you appropriately.

Practicing effective methods allows us to better understand ourselves. They also help us critically analyze and respond to the information presented, leading to more transparent communication exchanges.

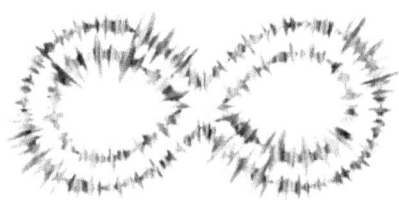

Comprehending Analytical Communication

Analytical communication entails the capability to express information clearly and effectively. This process conveys a message in an organized and coherent manner. It often uses data, evidence, and facts to support the relevant information. The ability to communicate analytically is vital in academic and professional settings, especially in scientific research, data analysis, problem-solving, and decision-making.

Benefits:
- Present complex ideas in a way that is easy to understand
- Support arguments and opinions with evidence
- Make well-informed decisions based on data
- Solve problems systematically by breaking them down into smaller components
- Convey information accurately and efficiently

Tips:
1. **Organize Your Thoughts:** Before communicating any information, take the time to structure it. Create an outline or framework to ensure your message is coherent.
2. **Use Data and Evidence:** Provide support for your arguments and ideas whenever possible. This will strengthen your material.
3. **Be Clear and Concise:** Avoid using jargon or unnecessary technical language. Instead, strive to communicate your ideas in a manner that is easy for others to understand.
4. **Practice Active Listening:** Be attentive during interactions and ask intentional questions. This active participation can make you feel more engaged in the communication process.
5. **Seek Feedback:** Consult a knowledgeable professional in this subject matter. This will ensure that you receive reliable advice.

Ryan Potter

Whether you are presenting a project, solving a problem, or making a persuasive argument, honing these skills can permit you to express information with clarity, precision, and depth. Practicing clear, logical, and evidence based communication enhances your ability to convey information accurately, empowering you to succeed in all your endeavors.

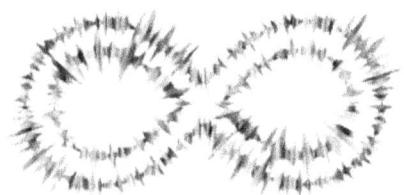

Critical Thinking

Critical thinking in communication with oneself involves analyzing our thoughts, feelings, beliefs, and values rationally. Practicing this evidence-based discipline enhances our understanding of ourselves and the world around us.

Being aware of our cognitive biases and distortions is fundamental. Cognitive biases are inaccuracies in thinking that can affect our judgment. Cognitive distortions are irrational thoughts or beliefs that can negatively impact our emotions. Recognizing and challenging these behavioral patterns improves the quality of our internal conversations.

Asking intentional questions is priceless. Set aside a few minutes each day for self-reflection. During this time, ask yourself questions such as "When did I start to believe this?" or "What evidence supports this thought?" Doing this enables you to uncover underlying assumptions and misconceptions.

Actively consider alternative viewpoints to broaden your perspective. Becoming more open-minded can lead to more refined and mindful internal dialogues.

Distinguish between facts and opinions. Facts are objective, verifiable statements about the world. Opinions are subjective, personal beliefs or judgments. Evaluating the evidence supporting our beliefs helps us make more well-informed conclusions.

Evaluate the consequences of your thoughts and actions. It's like playing chess with our minds. We anticipate potential outcomes as well as consider the impact of our decisions on ourselves and others. This reflective process enables us to make choices that align with our values and goals.

Critical thinking equips us with the capability to recognize and challenge faulty inferences that may cloud our minds. Honing these skills enhances our self-awareness and improves our decision-making processes.

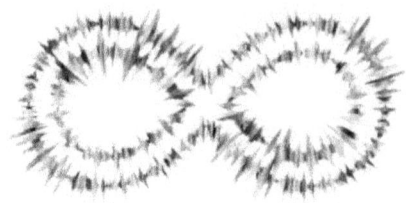

Intuitive Reasoning

At its core, intuitive reasoning is the ability to understand or know something without needing logical reasoning. It's like a hidden guide that helps us make sense of the world around us. It encompasses trusting our instincts, gut feelings, and emotions to make decisions.

In communication, we can notice nonverbal cues and grasp the underlying emotions behind words. However, interpreting the information we perceive through intuitive rationale can be challenging. The way we discern intuition can sometimes lead us astray.

When we rely on intuition, it can influence how we express ourselves, interpret messages from others, and affect the strength of our connections. Being open and receptive assists us in understanding the information we receive.

Impact:
- Intuitive reasoning acts as a powerful internal compass. It helps us tune into our thoughts, feelings, and needs without overanalyzing every detail. Tapping into intuition helps us better understand our emotions, motivations, and values.
- We can also engage in introspection by listening to our inner voice. Trusting our instincts helps us to make choices that align with our true selves.

Effect on Interpersonal Communication:
- Being attuned to intuition aids us in connecting with people on a deeper level. We can empathize with others, notice subtle cues, and respond to their needs.
- We can also establish rapport. Creating a communication dynamic based on genuine empathy deepens our connection with others.

Enhancing Intuitive Reasoning Skills:
- Develop the ability to trust your instincts. Work toward accurately reading nonverbal cues.
- Practice active listening, maintaining an open mind, and being emotionally aware.

Intuitive Reasoning

Harnessing intuition is a pathway to comprehending yourself and the world more profoundly. Developing intuitive reasoning skills can enhance communication effectiveness, leading to a more fulfilling life.

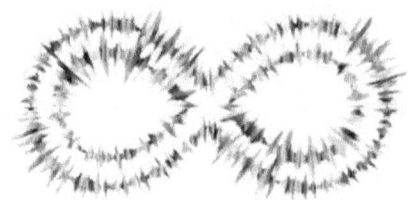

Logical Reasoning

Logical reasoning utilizes rational thinking and evidence to make sense of the world around us. While logical reasoning is a valuable skill that helps us analyze situations and solve problems, it can sometimes get in the way.

When we rely too heavily on logic, we may overlook our emotions, intuition, or deeper feelings. Ignoring ourselves can lead to a lack of awareness and understanding.

A Swiss psychologist named Jean Piaget is best known for his groundbreaking work in developmental psychology. One of his most significant contributions to psychology was his exploration of logical reasoning in the early 1900s.

Piaget observed that as children grow and develop, their ability to think logically and solve problems matures. His discovery of logical reasoning in psychology has had a lasting impact on the field, helping us unravel the complexities of human cognition and behavior.

Emotions are integral to who we are, offering valuable insights into our needs and desires. When prioritizing logical thinking over emotional awareness, we may suppress or dismiss our feelings as irrelevant. This can result in inner conflict, stress, and disconnection from ourselves.

Logical reasoning tends to categorize information into neat boxes of right or wrong without considering the complexity of human experience. When we apply this binary thinking to self-reflection, we may oversimplify our thoughts and behaviors while failing to see the underlying factors that influence them.

Constantly evaluating our thoughts or actions through what we perceive as a logical lens causes us to overlook the lessons our experiences can teach us. This critical inner voice can create a negative feedback loop that diminishes our sense of self-worth.

Common Limitations:

- **Cognitive Biases:** Cognitive biases are errors in thinking that affect our decisions and judgments. For example, confirmation bias leads people to favor information confirming their beliefs while ignoring evidence contradicting those beliefs. This can limit our ability to see the whole picture.

- **Emotional Influence:** Our emotions can cloud our judgment. We may ignore logical evidence that disagrees with our feelings when we feel strongly about something. This emotional influence can lead to irrational decisions.
- **Overgeneralization:** Sometimes, we may take one instance or a small amount of evidence and apply it too broadly. For example, if someone has a bad experience with a specific type of food, they might conclude that all similar foods are bad. This overgeneralization can lead to faulty reasoning.
- **Limited Information:** Making decisions with incomplete information can lead to poor reasoning. Without all the facts, we may jump to conclusions that are not well-founded.
- **Complexity of Issues:** Some problems are complex and involve many variables. Trying to simplify these issues can lead to misunderstandings and oversights.

Tips:
1. **Recognize Biases:** Educate yourself about common biases and reflect on your thought processes. When making a decision, ask yourself if you are considering all viewpoints or favoring information that supports your beliefs.
2. **Manage Emotions:** Take a moment to pause and assess your feelings before making a decision. Ask yourself if your emotions are influencing your judgment. Write down your thoughts to separate emotional responses from logical reasoning.
3. **Seek Diverse Perspectives:** Talk to people with different experiences or opinions. Gather a variety of viewpoints to help you see beyond your biases and broaden your understanding of an issue.
4. **Gather Comprehensive Information:** Conduct research, read articles, or consult experts in the field. The more informed you are, the better equipped you will be to make healthier decisions. Consider the credibility of your sources to ensure you are receiving accurate information.
5. **Break Down Complex Problems:** When faced with complex issues, break them into smaller, manageable parts. Analyze each component separately before considering how they interconnect. This systematic approach can help you avoid oversimplification and enable you to understand the intricacies of the problem.
6. **Use Logical Frameworks:** Tools such as flowcharts, decision trees, and pros and cons lists can help clarify your thoughts. These frameworks guide you through a structured process of evaluating information for analytical decisions.
7. **Reflect on Past Decisions:** Analyze what worked well and what didn't. Did any biases or emotional influences affect your conclusions? Learning from past experiences can help you strengthen your reasoning skills in the future.

Ryan Potter

While logical reasoning is a valuable tool for making sense of the world, knowing its limitations is indispensable. Balancing logic with emotional intelligence deepens our understanding of ourselves. Embracing the complexity of our inner experiences can lead to greater authenticity, connection, and personal growth.

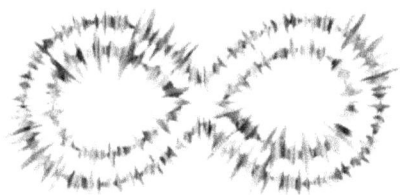

Bias Versus Distortion

Two concepts that are integral in how we decipher information are cognitive bias and cognitive distortion. While these terms may sound similar, they refer to psychological phenomena that can influence our thoughts and decision-making processes in distinct ways.

Cognitive bias is a systematic pattern that diverges from logical reasoning. They can impact how we interpret information from the external world, leading to errors in our judgment. Conclusions about other people and situations may be drawn in an unreasonable manner.

There are many types of cognitive biases. They can affect anyone, regardless of intelligence. These beliefs often stem from our brain's attempt to simplify information processing.

Cognitive distortion is an internal thought pattern that alters how we perceive reality. These distortions are often negative and irrational beliefs individuals hold about themselves, their experiences, and the world around them.

These unrealistic perspectives can cause emotional distress, contributing to conditions like anxiety or depression. Understanding these misconceptions can urge individuals to take proactive steps toward improving their mental health.

The primary distinction between cognitive bias and cognitive distortion is their effects on cognition. Cognitive biases can skew our decision-making by influencing how we process information. On the other hand, cognitive distortions misrepresent reality by altering our perceptions and affecting our emotional responses.

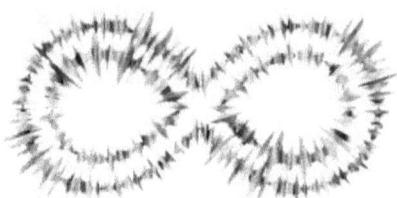

Grasping Cognitive Bias

Cognitive bias refers to how our brains can sometimes lead us to make decisions that are not based on evidence. The exploration of cognitive biases dates back to the early 1970s when psychologists Amos Tversky and Daniel Kahneman began their groundbreaking research.

More than 180 cognitive biases can shape our beliefs and attitudes. Being aware of them can help us think more critically. It is important to note that cognitive biases differ from making a mistake. They consist of a persistent pattern of deviation from rationality. Understanding these biases can prevent less-than-optimal outcomes.

Common Cognitive Biases:
1. **Confirmation bias** involves reinforcing beliefs by searching for, interpreting, favoring, or remembering information that confirms preexisting hypotheses. Doing so enables people to overlook, downplay, or dismiss information contradicting their beliefs.

    For example, suppose someone believes that eating healthy food is expensive. In that case, they may only focus on the high prices of organic products while ignoring the affordability of other nutritious options. To counteract this bias, seek out diverse perspectives and consider all available evidence before deciding on a conclusion.

2. **Sampling bias** is collected in such a way that it is not representative of the entire population, leading to inaccurate or misleading results. This can happen if certain groups are more likely to be included in the sample than others.

    Consider a survey about favorite ice cream flavors conducted at a vanilla-only ice cream shop. The results would be biased because they do not reflect the general population's preferences. Reflecting the diversity within a population ensures that research findings are more reliable.

3. **Brilliance bias** is where people believe that success is linked to natural talent or exceptional intelligence while overlooking other important factors like hard work, dedication, or perseverance. It can lead to underestimating one's potential or the abilities of others who may not fit the traditional image of "brilliance."

    True success often comes from a combination of various skills, experiences, and efforts rather than just innate brilliance. Understanding and challenging this bias helps create a more inclusive environment where everyone's unique contributions are valued.

4. **Actor-observer bias** is a tendency for people to attribute their actions to internal factors while attributing other people's behaviors to external factors. This bias often occurs because we have more information about the circumstances influencing our behavior compared to the details we have about others.

    For example, suppose we do well on a test. We might attribute that situation to our hard work and intelligence. If someone else does well, we might attribute it to luck or claim their test was easy. Recognizing this bias can aid us in comprehending how we interpret actions.

5. **Authority bias** is when individuals trust the ideas and actions of authority figures, such as teachers, parents, or experts, without critically evaluating them. This bias can influence the decisions we make, leading people to accept information as accurate simply because it comes from someone in a position of authority. It's vital to assess information, regardless of its source.

6. **Hindsight bias** leads us to believe that events are more predictable after they have already occurred. This is often referred to as the "I knew it all along" phenomenon. In other words, it's the tendency to discern past events as having been more predictable than they actually were before they happened.

    This bias can distort our memories of past decisions or judgments, making us believe we knew the outcome all along, even when we didn't. It's essential to learn from our experiences so that we can make sound decisions in the future.

7. **Anchoring bias** occurs when individuals rely primarily on the first piece of data they receive when making decisions. This initial information, or "anchor," influences their subsequent thoughts and judgments. Recognizing this bias can ensure that choices are made based on all available information.

8. **Attentional bias** focuses more on certain things while ignoring others. This bias can affect how we perceive information in our environment.

    For example, someone who is biased toward negative information may pay more attention to criticism rather than positive stimuli. Understanding this bias can impact our thoughts and emotions, which influence the behaviors we exhibit to the rest of the world.

9. **Anthropic bias** is a concept that explores how our observations about the universe may be influenced by the fact that we exist as humans. It questions if our presence affects how we perceive the world around us.

   For example, when considering the likelihood of certain conditions in the universe, we need to consider that our existence could impact our perspective. This idea challenges us to think critically about how our presence may shape our understanding of the universe and the probabilities we assign to different outcomes.
10. **Distinction bias** happens when we perceive two options as more different from each other than they actually are instead of objectively evaluating their true qualities. For example, we might focus on one feature that stands out on a more expensive phone while overlooking the overall value of a cheaper option. Considering all the facts without being swayed by superficial differences can help us make more educated decisions.
11. **In-group bias** gives preferential treatment to group members over those considered to be a part of an out-group. Shared characteristics, such as affiliations or beliefs, can lead to loyalty, pride, and a sense of belonging within the in-group while potentially causing stereotypes, prejudice, or discrimination towards members outside the group.
12. **Negativity bias** focuses more on negative information or experiences than positive ones. Think of it as having a built-in "lean towards the gloomy" default setting. It can impact our emotions, decisions, and overall outlook on life.
13. **Optimism bias** refers to individuals who believe they are less likely to experience unfavorable results than others. This can lead people to underestimate risks and overestimate the possibility of positive outcomes. While it can boost confidence and motivation, a realistic assessment of risks encourages well-informed decisions.
14. **Pessimism bias** is a way of thinking where individuals tend to focus more on the adverse conditions of a situation. This bias can lead people to always expect the worst outcomes, even when evidence suggests otherwise. Someone might automatically assume that they will fail even if they have worked hard or performed well in the past.
15. **Self-serving bias** is a propensity for individuals to view themselves optimistically by attributing positive events to their character or actions and adverse events to external factors. It enables us to protect ourselves by maintaining a positive self-image. For example, if you do well on a project, you might attribute it to your intelligence and hard work. However, if you perform poorly, you might blame the project for being too complicated or the manager for not explaining the material well.

16. **Belief bias** occurs when someone's preexisting sentiments influence their reasoning process. For example, someone who firmly believes that all dogs are friendly may incorrectly assume that a barking dog they encounter will not bite. It's imperative to consciously separate personal opinions from objective facts when evaluating information or making judgments.
17. **Bias blind spot** encompasses the habit of individuals seeing themselves as less biased than others while recognizing bias in other people. People often believe that they are more objective and impartial in their judgments and decision-making than they actually are. This makes it challenging to overcome prejudices and predispositions.

Mental shortcuts can significantly impact our daily lives. These viewpoints are not a sign of weakness or incompetence. They are a natural part of human cognition. Becoming more aware of these preferences helps us consider alternative perspectives and make more rational choices.

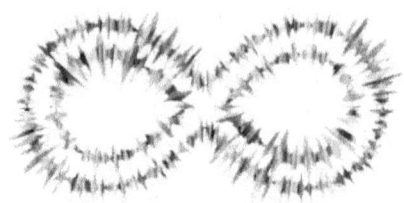

Sensing Cognitive Distortions

Have you ever had thoughts that seem to make you anxious or upset without solid evidence to back them up? This type of inner dialogue is known as cognitive distortions. These unreasonable thought patterns often reinforce negative thinking, leading to inner turmoil. Recognizing when they occur can help us regain balance in our lives.

The concept of cognitive distortions was first introduced by the renowned psychiatrist Aaron T. Beck in the 1960s. Beck is often referred to as the father of cognitive therapy. He noticed that his patients with depression had skewed perspectives of themselves, the world, and the future.

This groundbreaking research paved the way for cognitive-behavioral therapy (CBT). It's a highly effective form of psychotherapy that aids individuals in examining viewpoints that are causing them emotional distress. These mental processes are like tricks our minds play on us. They can lead us to make incorrect assumptions based on limited information.

Types:
- **Black-and-white thinking** involves seeing things as only one extreme or the other. It's also known as all-or-nothing thinking or polarized thinking. Things are either right or wrong, with no room for anything in between.

    Ignoring the complexities of life can cause misunderstandings. This lack of flexibility contributes to perfectionism and dissatisfaction. Most things in life fall into a gray area with multiple possibilities.
- **Overgeneralization** is a thinking error where someone makes a broad conclusion based on limited evidence. It happens when we apply one experience to all similar situations.

    Suppose someone has a bad experience with a particular type of food. In that case, they might think that all similar foods will taste bad. This mindset limits one's ability to see the bigger picture, leading to unfair judgments and stereotypes.

- **Catastrophizing** imagines the worst possible outcome for a situation and reacts as though it is inevitable. This can blow things out of proportion by making minor problems seem much more significant than they are. Someone might think, for instance, "If I fail at this, my life is over."
- **Magnification** exaggerates the importance of considerations. In other words, it's like using a magnifying glass to enlarge a tiny ant into a giant monster.
- **Minimization** underestimates the significance of something. People may downplay their achievements, ignore positive feedback, or diminish the impact of their actions on themselves and others.
- **Labeling** occurs when we attach generalizations to ourselves or others based on a specific characteristic. For example, calling yourself a "failure" because you made a mistake at work. Instead, recognize that everyone makes mistakes from time to time.
- **Discounting the positive** tends to overlook, downplay, or dismiss positive experiences, qualities, or achievements. Individuals may attribute their successes to luck or ignore them altogether, undermining their worth. For example, someone might receive a compliment on their work but brush it off as insignificant while dwelling on any criticism they receive.
- **Mental filtering** focuses only on the negative facets of a situation while ignoring or dismissing the positive ones. It's like wearing glasses that only let in lousy news. This misinterpretation can make people feel like everything is going wrong. Seeing the whole picture enables us to feel hopeful.
- **Emotional reasoning** happens when individuals believe their emotions accurately reflect objective reality regardless of the facts. In other words, people may feel like something is true because they feel it strongly, even if evidence suggests otherwise.

    For example, a person might believe they are unlikable because they feel lonely, even though their friends genuinely enjoy their company. Considering all of the facts promotes a more balanced perspective.
- **Should, must, and ought statements** often create pressure from unrealistic expectations. Individuals using these statements set themselves up for disappointment. For example, thinking "I should always perform perfectly" or "I must never make mistakes" can lead to stressful feelings.
- **Comparison** occurs when people judge their value based on how they stack up against others. This misrepresentation can lead to inadequacy, jealousy, or superiority. Focusing on perceived shortcomings or feeling envious of others' success can prevent us from appreciating our unique qualities and accomplishments.

- **Personalization** consists of taking responsibility for external events or outcomes, even when they are beyond someone's control. A person might believe they cause all the problems in a relationship. In reality, there are numerous other factors at play. This unwarranted thinking can lead to feelings of guilt or shame.
- **Blaming** is a defense mechanism in which individuals attribute the cause of a problem to someone else without considering their role in the situation or other reasons. They may engage in this behavior to protect their self-esteem.

    For example, someone might blame their project manager for performing poorly. Instead of taking ownership of their actions, they attribute fault to external factors. This can cause misunderstandings, strained relationships, and hindered problem-solving skills.
- **Jumping to conclusions** means quickly making assumptions or judgments without having all the necessary information. Rather than verifying details, individuals might make decisions based on their limited perspective. Gather all relevant data before forming an opinion. This distortion can manifest in two ways: mind reading and fortune telling.

    Mind reading takes effect when individuals believe they know what others think or feel, even when no evidence supports this assumption. This mentality relies on inaccurate perceptions rather than engaging in open communication.

    Fortune telling takes place when a person predicts that things will turn out badly without basis. People engaging in fortune telling might believe that they already know what will happen, which can lead to feelings of anxiety and hopelessness.
- **Always being right** arises when individuals believe their opinions, beliefs, or judgments are repeatedly correct. They tend to dismiss any contradictory evidence. A persistent need to be right in every situation can cause problems in communication. Individuals may become defensive or argumentative when faced with differing viewpoints.

Tips:
1. **Reality Testing:** Is this way of thinking based on facts or emotions?
2. **Developing Alternative Explanations:** What other perspectives could there be?
3. **Examining The Evidence:** What information supports or opposes this mentality?
4. **Behavioral Experiments:** Take small steps to see if your predictions are factual.

Our thoughts have a potent influence on our emotions and behaviors. Practice healthier thinking habits by challenging them. Intentional questions help us to see situations more realistically. Practicing this mindful approach trains our minds to think more rationally and improves our overall well-being.

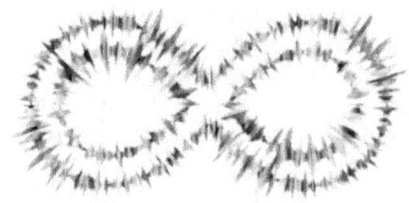

Asking Intentional Questions

Intentional questions are open-ended inquiries designed to encourage the receiver to reflect on thoughts or elaborate on a topic. These questions often start with words like "Who," "What," "When," "Where," or "How."

Studies have shown that when asked "why" questions, people tend to have strong emotional reactions and can feel triggered up to 60-70% of the time. Understanding questions that start with why and how they cause triggers can be traced back to the pioneering work of psychologist Dr. Rachel Smith in the early 20th century.

If you catch yourself asking a "why" question internally while alone or externally with others, continue by saying, "Let me rephrase that." Unlike closed-ended questions that elicit short answers, open-ended questions invite longer and more detailed responses.

Closed-ended questions are a type of questioning that can ordinarily be answered with a simple "yes," "no," or other specific short responses. The person being asked does not need to explain further. It makes them useful for gathering direct information. They often start with words like "Is," "Are," "Did," "Would," "Could," or "Have," and are commonly used in surveys, multiple-choice tests, or when seeking specific details. Familiarizing yourself with closed-ended questions can help you interact more effectively and efficiently in various settings.

Whether speaking with others or engaging in self-reflection, repeating the words used will help you obtain your desired information. You can reveal gaps in information, such as unknown motivations, fears, and desires that may impact thoughts and actions. For the following types of questioning, replace '...' with the relevant words of the desired information.

Clarification questions are used to clear up any ambiguity in the data provided.
- "Can you tell me more about '...'?"
- "What do you mean by '...'?"
- "Can you provide an example of '...'?"

Asking Intentional Questions

Expansion questions uncover additional details from initial responses.
- "How did '...' feel?"
- "How have your views changed over time regarding '...'?"
- "What challenges have you faced while working on '...'?"

Reflection questions prompt critical thinking about opinions, beliefs, or decisions.
- "What evidence is there to support '...'?"
- "How might '...' be viewed from another perspective?"
- "In what ways could '...' be improved?"

Tips:
1. **Set Aside Time:** Find a quiet and comfortable place to tend to your thoughts without distractions.
2. **Be Mindful:** Focus your full attention on understanding the message while offering empathy.
3. **Be Curious:** Approach the topic with a genuine interest in learning more.
4. **Start Broad:** Ask open-ended questions that encourage in-depth exploration. For example, "What are my core values?" or "What do I want to achieve in the next year?"
5. **Be Patient:** Permit a complete reply before continuing with more questions.
6. **Dig Deeper:** Ask follow-up questions about a topic of interest to explore it more. For instance, "How does this make me feel?"
7. **Avoid Leading Questions:** Steer clear of questions that suggest a particular answer.
8. **Encourage Storytelling:** Insights can be amplified.
9. **Challenge Assumptions:** Ask yourself, "Why do I have these beliefs?" and "Are they based on facts or emotions?"
10. **Use Nonverbal Cues:** Use positive body language. Maintain comfortable levels of eye contact.
11. **Be Honest:** Acknowledge your strengths and weaknesses based on evidence.
12. **Reflect on Actions:** Consider how your beliefs influence your behavior. Ask yourself what changes you can make to align your actions with your values.

Common Pitfalls to Avoid:
- **Self-Criticism:** The goal is not to criticize or judge yourself harshly. Instead, approach the process with curiosity and compassion.
- **Avoidance:** Don't shy away from exploring uncomfortable topics. Welcome them as an opportunity for growth.
- **Rigidity:** Be open to changing your beliefs based on new information.

Incorporating these tips into your self-reflection practice allows you to embark on a journey of self-discovery. Live a purposeful life by utilizing intentional questions and unlock your full potential.

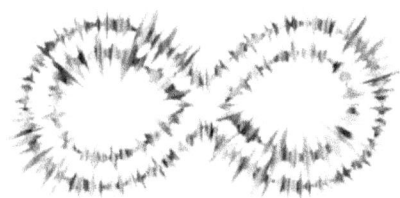

Self-Expression

The way we talk can either build us up or tear us down. Intentional and purposeful communication is a valuable mechanism for self-worth. Being tactful can positively impact performance in any situation.

Use "I" statements to assertively and respectfully express yourself. They begin with the word "I." Removing "you" from statements helps reduce the risk of appearing to place blame on others.

Examples:
- "I feel unheard when interrupted" instead of "They never listen to me."
- "I can overcome challenges" rather than "They always mess things up."
- "I will give it my best shot" alternatively to "I can't do this."

Understanding and revealing your limits is paramount. Say no when necessary. Practice using direct and honest "I" statements tactfully. This approach promotes constructive dialogue in taking ownership of your internal experiences.

Setting specific goals can guide your internal dialogue toward positive outcomes that align with your values. When aspiring toward an objective, utilize smart goals. Create a road map for success by breaking down your goals into small steps and monitoring your progress. Describe what you want to accomplish both short-term and long-term.

Clarifying your needs ensures your decisions are understood and valued. Communicating clearly can avoid misunderstandings. Developing practical self-expression skills can pave the way for efficient communication.

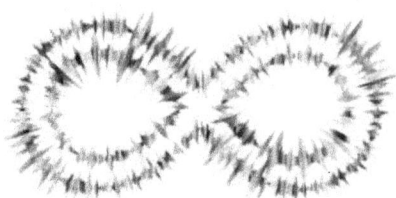

Efficient Communication

Developing efficient self-communication skills involves being clear and concise when conveying information. To communicate efficiently with yourself, it is paramount to consider the indispensable components of effective communication.

Engaging in thoughtful internal dialogue encourages us to evaluate different perspectives, anticipate obstacles, and produce creative solutions. When faced with difficult choices, listening to our inner thoughts and concerns can help us weigh our options.

Taking notes, setting alarms, scheduling appointments in your calendar, or texting reminders to yourself on your phone are some examples of when efficient self-communication is convenient. Streamlining processes can boost productivity by clearing our minds.

Tips:
1. **Keep It Simple:** Avoid overcomplicating your experiences. Organize your thoughts before speaking or writing. Stay on topic to ensure your message is easily understood. Avoid using vague language. Clarity helps prevent misunderstandings and ensures that your future self is on the same page as your past self.
2. **Utilize Visualization Techniques:** Create mental images of desired outcomes. Picture the steps needed for success. Mind maps, diagrams, and charts can help you organize your ideas and track your progress effectively.
3. **Practice Mindfulness:** Take a few minutes each day to reflect on your experiences. Meditation or deep breathing techniques can help quiet your inner critic. Concentrate on one thing at a time to reduce stress. Journaling can help you center your thoughts and improve the efficiency of constructive analysis.
4. **Take Breaks:** Prevent burnout. Participate in hobbies that provide you joy and relaxation. Return to your thoughts with a fresh perspective.

Give yourself the time to apply these strategies in your daily life and experience their profoundly positive influence. Doing so will boost self-esteem, enhance decision-making skills, and increase confidence in various aspects of life.

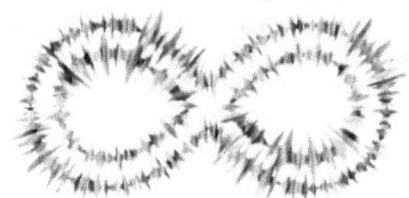

Boosting Confidence

Confidence is the conviction in oneself and one's abilities. It's like a muscle that can be strengthened through practice and effort. When individuals are confident in their capabilities, they are more likely to think outside the box. Believing in themselves allows them to explore new possibilities and produce innovative solutions.

Tips:
1. Clear your mind by creating a list.
2. Remind yourself of your strengths.
3. Accomplish the most straightforward tasks first. Then, work your way up to more complex objectives.
4. Take the time to practice what you need to do.
5. Visualize your success. Reflect on your progress.
6. Engage in activities that relax your mind and body.
7. Exercise, nutrition, and quality sleep can all contribute to how you feel.
8. Surround yourself with friends and family who encourage you.

Stepping out of one's comfort zone by trying new things can help overcome fears. Not every interaction or goal will go as planned on the first try. Being adaptable liberates us from our constraints.

This path of personal growth may not always be easy, but it is worth it. Practicing these tips helps us learn our worth. Overcoming challenges enables individuals to unlock new opportunities, form stronger connections, and lead more fulfilling lives.

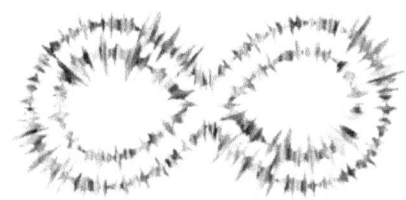

Expanding Imaginative Skills

Imagination allows us to create, innovate, and solve problems. It is the ability to form new images and ideas that are not present to our senses. Imaginative skills involve several components, including creativity, visualization, and innovative thinking.

Creativity is the ability to think of new and original ideas. Visualization is the ability to see things in your mind, like imagining a story or a picture before creating it. Innovative thinking refers to the process of coming up with solutions to problems in new and different ways.

Imaginative skills are not limited to artists or writers. Everyone can benefit from developing these skills. Scientists use imagination to hypothesize and create experiments. Engineers imagine how to build structures or design products. Even in everyday life, we use imaginative skills when planning a party, solving a conflict with a friend, or figuring out the best way to complete homework. Developing these abilities helps us become better at critical thinking.

Impact:
- **Self-Awareness:** Delve deep into your inner self.
- **Creativity:** Produce unique ideas and solutions.
- **Problem-Solving:** View situations from different angles.
- **Decision-Making:** Weigh the pros and cons of differing choices.
- **Increased Innovation:** Devise new products or services.
- **Communication:** Express yourself in engaging ways.
- **Flexibility:** Adapt to change by exploring different possibilities.
- **Stress:** Reduce stress by managing feelings more effectively.

Tips:
1. **Engage in Creative Activities:** To stimulate your imagination, try activities like drawing, painting, drafting stories, or composing music.
2. **Read Widely:** Reading books, especially fiction and fantasy genres, can expose you to new ideas.

3. **Daydream:** Allow yourself time to daydream and let your mind wander freely to produce creative ideas.
4. **Brainstorm:** Practice brainstorming sessions where you generate multiple ideas with compassion.
5. **Explore New Perspectives:** Challenge yourself to see things from different viewpoints to broaden your thinking.
6. **Play Games:** Play games that require strategy, problem-solving, or creativity.
7. **Journaling:** Write down thoughts, feelings, and reflections to help you practice self-expression.
8. **Visualization Techniques:** Engage in guided imagery and visualization exercises to help you explore different scenarios within your mind.
9. **Mindfulness Practices:** Activities like meditation and deep breathing can strengthen the connection between the mind and body.
10. **Conflict Resolution:** Consider different perspectives and find peaceful resolutions.
11. **Goal Setting:** Visualize aspirations to motivate you to achieve your objectives.

Imaginative skills enable us to modify our communication style to connect with diverse audiences. This ongoing process requires practice and exploration.

Embracing creativity, thinking outside the box, and nurturing your imagination can unlock new opportunities and upgrade your life in countless ways. Imagination has no limits. As you exercise it more, it will flourish and benefit you in all areas of your life.

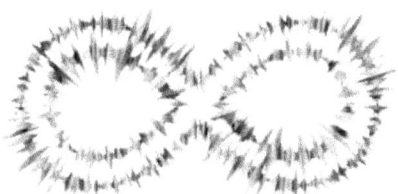

Black-and-White Thinking

Black-and-white thinking, also known as binary thinking, involves viewing situations, people, or oneself in strict and absolute terms. This type of thinking leaves no room for anything in between. Parmenides was one of the earliest known philosophers to discuss this type of thinking. He believed in the concept of the "One," where he argued that reality is unchanging and indivisible. He saw the world in binary terms - existence and non-existence.

Individuals who engage in rigid standards tend to set unrealistic expectations for themselves. This can lead to a profound sense of inadequacy, a crushing blow to self-esteem, and relentless self-criticism. For example, a student may believe that they are a complete failure if they don't get a perfect score on a test. This type of thinking can be paralyzing and prevent individuals from seeing their progress and achievements.

When individuals see things in absolutes, they may struggle to consider alternative perspectives or find flexible solutions. This can hinder effective self-reflection and growth. Instead of offering themselves compassion and understanding, individuals may engage in negative self-talk and harsh self-criticism. This internal dialogue can perpetuate feelings of stress, anxiety, and depression.

Common Signs:
- **All-or-Nothing Statements:** Phrases like "I always mess things up" or "I never do anything right" indicate an all-or-nothing mindset.
- **Labeling:** Calling yourself names such as "loser" or "failure" after making a mistake can show black-and-white thinking.
- **Overgeneralization:** Thinking that one negative experience means everything will go wrong in the future is another example.

Tips:
1. **Practice Mindfulness:** When you feel overwhelmed, take a moment to breathe deeply. Notice what you see, hear, and feel around you. This can help ground you and reduce the intensity of your emotions.

2. **Challenge Your Thoughts:** Ask questions to explore the gray areas when thinking in extremes.

    Examples:
    - What evidence do I have that supports this thought?
    - Are there other explanations for what I am experiencing?
    - What would I say to a friend who is thinking this way?

3. **Reframe Your Thoughts:** Instead of labeling yourself as a "failure" for not achieving a perfect score, recognize your effort and progress. For example, instead of saying, "I always mess up," you could say, "Sometimes I make mistakes, but I can learn from them." This slight shift in wording can significantly impact how you perceive yourself and your experiences.

4. **Use "And" Instead of "Or":** Instead of saying, "I am either a success or a failure," try saying, "I can be successful in some areas and still have room to improve in others." This way of thinking acknowledges that you can simultaneously have positive and negative experiences.

5. **Keep a Balanced Journal:** Write down situations in which you felt you were thinking in black-and-white terms. Next to each situation, write a more balanced thought.

    For example:
    - **Initial Thought:** "I didn't make the soccer team. I'm terrible at sports."
    - **Balanced Thought:** "I didn't make the team this time. I can try again next season. I enjoy playing soccer regardless."

6. **Focus on the Spectrum:** Create a list of potential outcomes for circumstances. For instance, if you receive a grade that isn't an A, consider all the possible levels of achievement, such as a B, C, or even a D, and reflect on what those grades represent regarding learning and effort.

7. **Set Realistic Expectations:** Focus on your progress. Allow yourself to celebrate small achievements along the way.

8. **Cultivate Self-Compassion:** Recognize that everyone faces challenges. It's okay to be imperfect. Doing the best that you can is what matters most.

9. **Seek Support:** Different perspectives help you see the bigger picture.

Life is rarely black and white. Embracing this complexity can lead to greater resilience, emotional intelligence, and overall well-being.

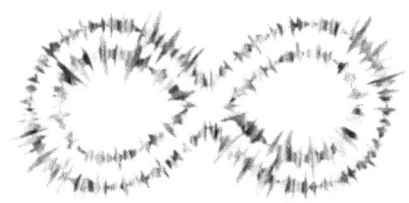

Overgeneralization

Overgeneralization involves taking one piece of evidence and applying it to all situations. A prominent psychologist named Jean Piaget first explored the concept in the 1960s. Painting a bleak and all-encompassing picture of ourselves can lead to a barrage of self-criticism, a plummet in self-esteem, and a perpetual feeling of defeat. Believing that failure is inevitable based on past experiences can hinder our ability to set and achieve goals.

Common Signs:
- **Using Absolute Words:** Overgeneralization often involves words like "always," "never," or "everyone." For instance, if you say, "I always mess up," you generalize one mistake to all your experiences.
- **Focusing on the Negative:** You may be overgeneralizing if you only remember the bad experiences and ignore the good ones. For example, if you only remember the times you felt sad and not the times you felt happy, you might think happiness is not possible.
- **Ignoring Exceptions:** If you find yourself thinking that because one bad thing happened, it will happen again, you are likely overgeneralizing. Recognize that not every situation is the same. If someone faces rejection in a relationship, they might convince themselves they are unlovable and destined for a lifetime of unhappiness.

Tips:
1. **Challenge Your Thoughts:** When using absolute language, ask yourself if it is true. Try to find exceptions. Recall times when you did something well. This can help you see that your thoughts are not always accurate.
    Examples:
    - What evidence do I have that supports this thought?
    - Have I had experiences that contradict this belief?
    - Am I using extreme language that might not be true?

- Are there factors that made me struggle this time that do not apply in general?
2. **Reframing the Situation:** Replace negative thoughts with positive affirmations. Instead of saying, "I always fail," try saying, "I can learn from my mistakes."
3. **Keep a Journal:** Brainstorm several alternative perspectives. Write down both the negative thought and the evidence against it. Listing your achievements can help. For example, instead of writing, "I never get good grades," write, "I did not do well on this test, but I can improve next time."
4. **Practice Mindfulness:** Take a moment to breathe. Observe your thoughts and feelings. This can provide greater clarity and calmness.
5. **Set Realistic Goals:** For example, if someone struggles with math, they might strive to practice it for 15 minutes each day rather than expecting to master all concepts immediately.
6. **Learn from Mistakes:** Reflect on what went wrong and how to improve next time.
7. **Seek Feedback:** Sometimes, we are too hard on ourselves, and a supportive person can remind us of our strengths. Negative experiences do not define your capabilities.

Consider joining support groups of people experiencing similar challenges. Sharing stories and strategies can help normalize feelings and provide additional coping mechanisms.

Instead of leaping to extreme conclusions based on limited evidence, adopt a more balanced and realistic view of your abilities and worth. This shift can bolster our self-confidence, resilience, and overall well-being.

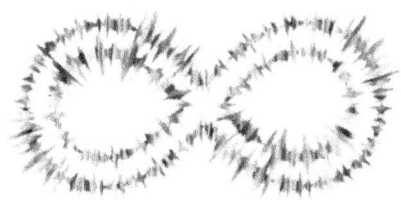

Labeling

Labeling assigns rigid and often harsh labels based on actions, thoughts, or characteristics. Labeling ourselves or allowing others to label us can significantly influence how we perceive ourselves, others, and the world around us.

Instead of embracing the complexity and variability of human behavior and emotions, we categorize ourselves as either "good" or "bad," "smart" or "stupid," "successful" or "failure." These labels, while seemingly simple, can be self-limiting as well as damaging.

This theory can be traced back to the early 20th century, when scholars began to explore how societal labels impact human behavior, particularly in criminology. Frank Tannenbaum is one of the prominent figures credited with the discovery of labeling theory in psychology. He argued that labeling someone as a criminal can result in that individual adopting the behaviors and identity associated with the label.

When we consistently label ourselves in a certain way, whether positive or negative, we start to internalize that label as part of our identity. Instead of offering ourselves compassion and understanding, we reinforce these harmful labels, creating a cycle of self-doubt and low self-worth. This can lead to anxiety, depression, perfectionism, and difficulties in forming healthy relationships with oneself and others.

Labels can also influence our emotional responses to situations. For instance, if individuals constantly label themselves as "anxious," they may be more likely to approach challenging situations with fear. This can conceive a self-fulfilling prophecy where the label itself reinforces the feeling of anxiety.

Labeling can result in a fixed mindset, where individuals believe their abilities and traits are static and cannot be changed. This mindset hinders personal growth and resilience, as individuals may avoid challenges or opportunities for fear of confirming their negative labels. It can lead to selective attention to information that aligns with these labels.

Labeling ourselves "lazy" or "unmotivated" may make us more inclined to procrastinate or avoid challenging tasks. These labels can become self-imposed barriers that hinder personal growth and achievement.

Tips:
1. **Challenge Negative Thoughts:** When you notice a negative label creeping into your mind, pause and ask yourself intentional questions.

    Examples:
    - Is this thought based on facts, or is it an opinion?
    - Would I say this to a friend in a similar situation?
    - What evidence do I have that contradicts this label?

2. **Practice Self-Compassion:** If you make a mistake, you might say, "I am learning, and this is part of my growth."
3. **Focus on Specific Behaviors, Not Labels:** For instance, if you didn't do well on a test, you might say, "I didn't study enough for this test," instead of labeling yourself as a failure. This shift in language allows you to see areas for improvement.
4. **Embrace Challenges:** Instead of avoiding strenuous tasks, view them as growth opportunities. Every challenge can teach you something new.
5. **Learn From Criticism:** Constructive feedback can be valuable. Rather than seeing it as a personal attack, view it as a chance to improve.
6. **Celebrate Effort, Not Just Results:** Recognize that the effort you put into learning truly matters. Celebrate your hard work, even if the outcome isn't perfect.
7. **Use Positive Affirmations:** Rewire your brain to focus on your strengths rather than weaknesses. Establish a list of affirmations that resonate with you. Some could include "I am capable of learning" or "I am doing my best." Repeat these affirmations daily, especially when you feel negative thoughts creeping in. Over time, positive affirmations can help replace the negative labels with a more optimistic perspective.

    Examples:
    - "I am capable of learning and growing."
    - "I am more than my mistakes."
    - "I can improve my skills with effort."

    Positive labels such as "kind" or "hardworking" can boost self-esteem and lead to more confident self-talk. Adopting labels such as "resilient" or "calm" can help us approach difficulties with a more positive mindset. Labels like "determined" or "persistent" can instill a sense of perseverance and drive us to overcome obstacles.

8. **Engage in Reflective Journaling:** Take time each day to write about your thoughts and feelings. When you notice a negative label, write it down and then challenge it with evidence that contradicts it.

9. **Limit Comparisons:** In today's world, measuring ourselves to others is easy, especially with social media. However, comparing ourselves to others can lead to negative labeling. Remind yourself that everyone has unique strengths and weaknesses. Focus on your journey and achievements rather than measuring yourself against someone else.
10. **Seek Feedback:** You are not alone. You can join groups or workshops that focus on building self-esteem and positive thinking.

You are more than the labels you assign yourself. Recognize that a single mistake or challenge does not define who we are. It's how we learn and grow that truly matters.

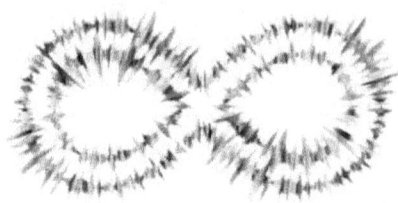

Catastrophizing

Catastrophizing consists of believing that if something bad can happen, it will happen. The concept of catastrophizing can be traced back to psychology, particularly to the work of American psychologist Albert Ellis in the 1950s.

When people catastrophize, they tend to focus on the worst possible outcomes. Magnifying unfortunate possibilities causes them to believe that minor issues are insurmountable. As a result, it can lead to heightened levels of fear, worry, and self-doubt.

Instead of approaching challenges with a clear and rational mindset, individuals may become overwhelmed by catastrophic thoughts, leading to a cycle of negative self-talk and rumination. This can hinder the individual's problem-solving skills and prevent them from considering alternative perspectives or solutions.

Constantly engaging in catastrophic thinking can erode confidence, breed feelings of helplessness, and intensify feelings of stress and anxiety. This can create substantial barriers to effective expression and compassion.

Tips:
1. **Challenge Your Thoughts:** For example, if you think, "I'll fail this test," consider your past performance and how much effort you have put in. This can help you realize that while the situation may be challenging, it is not hopeless. Ask yourself the following questions.
    - Is this thought based on facts or assumptions?
    - What evidence do I have that supports this thought?
    - What evidence do I have that contradicts it?
2. **Reframe Your Thoughts:** Change the way you perceive a situation. Instead of thinking, "I am going to fail this test," try rephrasing it to, "I didn't study as much as I wanted, but I can still do my best." When reframing, focus on the positive aspects and potential solutions rather than the negatives. This not only reduces anxiety but also empowers you to take action.
3. **Practice Self-Compassion:** Understand that everyone has tough days or experiences setbacks.

4. **Practice Mindfulness:** When you notice negative thoughts arise, take a moment to breathe deeply and focus on what is happening around you.

   Try this exercise:
   - **Find a quiet place** to get comfortable.
   - **Close your eyes** and take a few deep breaths, inhaling through your nose for a pace of three to six seconds and exhaling through your mouth for a pace of three to six seconds.
   - **Focus on your breath**. If your mind wanders, gently bring your attention back to your breathing.
   - **Utilize guided imagery**. Think about a scene or experience that makes you feel relaxed and happy. It could be a beach, a forest, or even a favorite memory. The more detailed your image, the better.
   - **Engage your senses**. What do you see? What sounds do you hear? What do you feel? Engaging your senses will make the experience more vivid.

5. **Focus on What You Can Control:** Make a list of aspects of the situation that you can control.
6. **Focus on Solutions:** Ask yourself what steps you can take to improve the situation. Taking action can empower you and reduce feelings of helplessness.

   For example, if you are worried about a low grade, consider:
   - Studying more effectively
   - Asking for help from a teacher or tutor
   - Joining a study group

7. **Limit Exposure to Negative Influences:** External factors can contribute to catastrophizing. Social media, negative news, or toxic relationships can amplify anxious thoughts. Consider taking breaks from social media or surrounding yourself with positive, supportive individuals who encourage healthy thinking.
8. **Seek Support:** Talking to someone can provide reassurance by helping you see things from a different angle. When discussing with others, try to express your thoughts and feelings.

   For example, you could say, "I'm feeling anxious about my upcoming presentation, and I keep thinking it will go horribly." Sharing your worries can often lighten the load and help you realize that you are not alone.

It's normal to have negative thoughts from time to time. Embracing these techniques can increase confidence, resilience, and overall success in life.

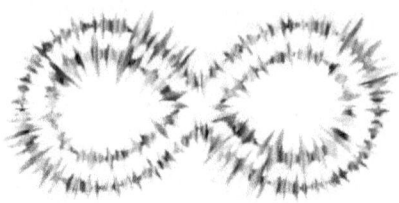

Magnification

Magnification pertains to making minor issues seem more significant than they are. Sigmund Freud's exploration of magnification, such as the concept of defense mechanisms in 1894, stemmed from his interest in understanding the unconscious mind.

Denial is a defense mechanism where an individual refuses to accept the reality of a situation. Freud believed that defense mechanisms often magnify certain facets of our thoughts and emotions, which can profoundly influence our behavior.

For instance, imagine a student receiving a less than perfect test grade. They may magnify this one failure, thinking, "I'm such a failure. I'll never be good at this," and ignore all the times they have succeeded in the past. This thinking can lead to feelings of inadequacy, self-doubt, and a distorted perception of one's abilities.

Magnification can also affect how we interpret feedback from others. When engaging in self-communication, individuals experiencing magnification may hyper-focus on criticism or negative comments, ignoring any positive feedback that may also be present. This rumination can create a cycle of negative self-talk and a distorted view of an individual's self-worth.

When faced with challenging situations, individuals who magnify the negative aspects may become overwhelmed and struggle to see potential solutions. This can hinder effective communication with oneself, leading to increased stress and anxiety.

Common Signs:
- **Exaggerated Negative Outcomes:** When you predict something terrible will happen, such as failing a class or disappointing others, without considering any evidence to support that prediction.
- **Overgeneralizing:** Making broad statements based on a single event, like thinking, "I always mess things up" after one mistake.
- **Ignoring the Positive:** Focusing only on the negatives and forgetting any positive aspects of a situation or your abilities.

Tips:
1. **Identify the Thought:** Write down the negative thought you are having. For example, "I always mess up."
2. **Gather Evidence:** Look for evidence that supports or contradicts this thought. Ask yourself, "Is this true?" and "What other evidence do I have?"
3. **Reframe the Thought:** Replace the negative thought with a more balanced one. Instead of saying, "I always mess up," you could say, "Sometimes I make mistakes, but I also succeed."
4. **Focus on the Present:** Magnification often involves worrying about the future or ruminating on the past.
5. **Deep Breathing:** Take slow breaths to relax your mind. Inhale for four counts, hold for four counts, then exhale for four counts. This will allow you to focus on the here and now, which can reduce anxiety.
6. **Mindful Observation:** Pay attention to the colors, sounds, and sensations around you for a few minutes. This method can shift your focus away from unproductive thoughts.
7. **Gratitude Journaling:** Write down three things you appreciate daily. This encourages you to accept the positive aspects of your life.
8. **Focus on Problem-Solving:** When faced with a challenging situation, focus on possible solutions instead of dwelling on the concern. Instead of thinking, "I can't handle this," ask yourself, "What steps can I take to make this better?" This proactive approach can help you feel more in control and less overwhelmed.
9. **Acknowledge Your Feelings:** Recognize that feeling upset or anxious is okay. Everyone experiences difficult emotions. Acknowledging them is the first step toward healing.
10. **Treat Yourself Like a Friend:** Comfort yourself with kindness and understanding.
11. **Set Realistic Goals:** Don't aim for perfection. Celebrate your successes, no matter how small they may seem.
12. **Seek Support:** Look for positive and motivational content that encourages a healthy mindset. Join a group where you can share stories with others facing similar challenges. This can create a sense of community and understanding. Consider speaking with a mental health professional. They can offer coping strategies to help you manage your thoughts.

Be patient with yourself as you work through these strategies. With time and effort, you can learn to see the bigger picture.

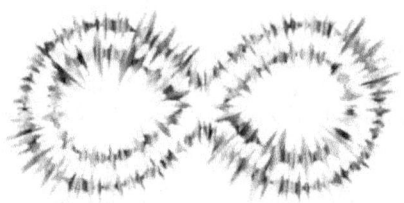

Minimization

Minimization tends to downplay the significance of positive events or attributes. The discovery of this distortion can be attributed to the pioneering work of psychologist Solomon Asch in the 1950s.

When individuals engage in minimization, they often struggle to acknowledge their accomplishments, strengths, and positive qualities. For example, someone who receives praise for a job well done may brush it off as insignificant, attributing their success to luck rather than their skills or efforts.

In many societies, there's a cultural norm of modesty toward one's achievements. Discounting positive feedback or experiences causes individuals to develop a skewed view of themselves and their abilities. This lack of recognition can cause feelings of inadequacy and self-doubt as individuals focus more on their perceived shortcomings rather than their achievements.

Individuals who consistently minimize their achievements or positive traits miss opportunities to celebrate progress and build confidence. Instead, they may engage in harmful comparisons with others or set unrealistic standards for themselves, leading to feelings of dissatisfaction and frustration.

Dismissing their successes or strengths may cause individuals to underestimate their capabilities and overlook potential solutions to challenges. This can limit their ability to overcome obstacles and adapt to new situations.

Tips:
1. **Acknowledge Your Feelings:** Instead of telling yourself your emotions do not matter, try expressing them. Write down your thoughts in a journal.

    For example, if you feel anxious about a presentation, instead of saying, "It's not a big deal," acknowledge your anxiety by writing, "I feel nervous about presenting, and that's okay." Recognizing your feelings is an integral part of the healing process.

2. **Challenge Negative Thoughts:** For example, if you think, "I didn't do much to deserve this award," you can challenge that thought by asking yourself, "What did I do to earn this award?" List the efforts that contributed to your success. This practice helps to reinforce the truth of your accomplishments.
3. **Practice Self-Compassion:** Recognize your worth. Take a moment each day to acknowledge a small success or treat yourself to something you enjoy.
4. **Set Realistic Goals:** Instead of minimizing your efforts, create specific, achievable goals that reflect your capabilities. Monitor your progress. Build confidence by celebrating small victories along the way.
5. **Reflect on Past Achievements:** Strengthen your belief in your abilities by thinking back to times when you succeeded or overcame challenges.
6. **Keep a Success Journal:** Write down your accomplishments, no matter how small they may seem. When feelings of minimization arise, you can revisit your journal to remind yourself of your capabilities.
7. **Practice Mindfulness:** Focus on your breath. Gently remind yourself that your feelings and efforts matter.
8. **Utilize Positive Affirmations:** Repeat affirmations like "My feelings are valid."
9. **Limit Negative Influences:** If you find yourself in situations where your achievements are consistently downplayed, limiting exposure to those influences may be beneficial.
10. **Seek Support:** Spend time with supportive friends, family, or mentors to make a significant difference. If you find it difficult to overcome minimization on your own, consider seeking help from a counselor or therapist.

Your emotions and achievements are valid. Recognizing your value is an indispensable step towards a healthier mindset and a more fulfilling life.

Discounting the Positive

Have you ever found yourself brushing off compliments or positive feedback? Discounting the positive refers to the tendency to downplay or ignore our accomplishments and strengths. Its discovery can be attributed to the pioneering work of psychologist Philip Brickman and his colleagues in the 1970s.

Instead of acknowledging and internalizing the positive aspects, individuals focus solely on the negative aspects. This distortion can manifest in several ways, such as deflecting admiration, dismissing achievements, or attributing success to external factors.

As a result, our worth is replaced by self-limiting beliefs. Constantly undermining our positive aspects paves the way for feelings of inadequacy, low self-esteem, and heightened self-criticism.

When we fail to recognize our strengths and successes, we may lack the confidence and motivation to pursue our aspirations. This can hinder our progress and keep us from reaching our full potential.

This distorted communication can perpetuate negative thought patterns and reinforce harmful beliefs about one's abilities. Thankfully, there are concrete strides we can take to combat the detrimental effects of discounting the positive.

Tips:
1. **Acknowledge Your Achievements:** When you accomplish something, no matter how small, take a moment to celebrate it. Keep a journal where you write down your successes, positive feedback from others, or moments when you felt proud of yourself. It could be a good grade on a paper, completing a project on time, or even helping a friend.

    Revisiting your success journal regularly can help you reinforce positive thinking. This practice can help you see the good things in your life and remind you that you can succeed.
2. **Recognize and Challenge Negative Thoughts:** Pay attention to your inner dialogue. Are you quick to dismiss compliments or ignore your achievements? When you notice these thoughts, challenge them.

Ask yourself:
- Is this thought based on facts?
- Am I overlooking evidence that supports my success?
- Would I say the same thing to a friend in my situation?

Replace destructive thoughts with more balanced ones. For example, instead of saying, "I got lucky on that test," reframe it to, "I studied hard and earned that grade." This shift in thinking can help you appreciate your efforts and achievements more fully.

3. **Practice Gratitude:** Take a few minutes each day to consider what you are thankful for. Write in a journal where you list three things you are grateful for each day. This could include personal achievements, supportive friends, or even small joys, like a sunny day or a favorite book.

4. **Use Positive Affirmations:** Repeat these affirmations daily, especially during moments of self-doubt. Over time, this practice can help build your self-esteem and reduce the tendency to discount positive experiences.

   Examples:
   - "I am proud of my efforts and achievements."
   - "I deserve to celebrate my successes."
   - "Every small step I take is important."

5. **Set Realistic Goals:** For instance, if your goal is to improve in math, instead of only focusing on getting an A, celebrate each quiz or homework assignment you complete. Acknowledging these smaller successes will help you see your positive progress.

6. **Focus on the Process, Not Just the Outcome:** We often focus too much on the results of our efforts rather than the effort itself. When you complete a task, reflect on the process you went through, including the hard work and dedication you put in.

   For example, if you finish a project, instead of solely focusing on your grade, think about the skills you developed and the lessons you learned along the way. Focus on the journey can help you appreciate your efforts more fully.

7. **Limit Comparisons with Others:** Everyone has a unique journey. Concentrate on your progress and personal milestones.

8. **Seek Support:** Receive feedback from friends, family, or teachers who uplift you. When someone compliments you or acknowledges your hard work, accept it graciously. Instead of brushing it off, say thank you and reflect on their words. This helps reinforce positive beliefs about yourself.

Everyone experiences moments of self-doubt. Embrace the good in your life, and your outlook will become more hopeful.

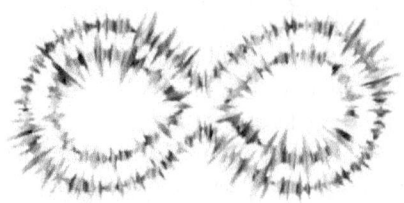

Mental Filtering

Mental filtering focuses exclusively on a situation's negative factors. The discovery of mental filtering in psychology can be attributed to the groundbreaking efforts of Aaron T. Beck, a renowned psychologist and the founder of cognitive therapy in the 1960s.

During any mental filtering engagement, we essentially "filter out" any information that contradicts our beliefs. When we consistently focus on our shortcomings, we reinforce negative perceptions about ourselves. This can erode our self-esteem, confidence, and overall mental well-being.

For example, if someone receives positive feedback on a project but chooses to focus only on one negative comment, they are engaging in mental filtering. This concentration can lead to a cycle of negative self-talk, feelings of inadequacy, and limited self-awareness, which can significantly impact our personal and professional lives.

We risk overlooking valuable insights or solutions if we disregard a situation's positive aspects. This can impede our personal growth and development.

Tips:
1. **Awareness and Acknowledgment:** Pay attention to your thoughts and feelings.
   Ask yourself questions like:
   - What negative thoughts am I having right now?
   - Am I ignoring any positive aspects of this situation?
   - How would I view this situation if I were being more objective?
2. **Reality Check:**
   Ask yourself:
   - What evidence do I have to support my thoughts?
   - What would I tell a friend if they were in my situation?
   - Can I find a more balanced or realistic perspective?
3. **Reframe Your Thoughts:** Look at the situation from different perspectives. For example, if you didn't do well on a test, instead of thinking, "I'm a failure," you could reframe it to, "I didn't do as well as I wanted, but I can learn from my mistakes."

4. **Focus on the Bigger Picture:** Evaluate situations from a broader viewpoint.
    Consider the following:
    - How vital is this situation in the grand scheme of things?
    - What will I think about this situation in a week or a month?
    - Are there other factors or perspectives I should consider?
5. **Positive Affirmations:**
    Examples:
    - "I am capable of learning and improving."
    - "I have many strengths that I can build on."
    - "I am worthy of success and happiness."
6. **Practice Gratitude:** Take a few minutes each day to write down three things you are thankful for. They can be big or small.
7. **Seek Support:** When you share your experiences, you may find that others have similar feelings and can offer advice or encouragement. Participate in group discussions or support groups.

The goal is not to ignore negative thoughts. It's to acknowledge them while also recognizing the positives. This grounds us in a more stable and resilient mental state.

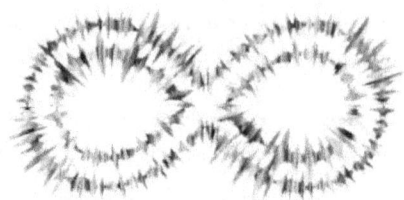

Emotional Reasoning

Emotional reasoning refers to using one's feelings as the primary basis for interpreting situations rather than relying on factual evidence. This concept was explored in the early 20th century when American psychologist Albert Ellis began developing cognitive behavioral therapy (CBT) theories.

Those who engage in excessive emotional reasoning often struggle with low self-esteem, as they constantly interpret their emotions as reflections of their inadequacies or failures. This detrimental perspective can substantially decline their mental health and overall well-being.

Individuals who prioritize their emotions over logical rationale can make impulsive decisions or avoid situations that trigger them. While emotional reasoning is a natural part of the human experience, healthy coping mechanisms help navigate its influence on self-communication.

Common Signs:
- **Strong Negative Feelings:** You feel overwhelmed by sadness, anxiety, or anger.
- **Thought Patterns:** Notice if you think in absolutes, like "I will never succeed" or "Nobody likes me."
- **Physical Symptoms:** Sometimes, emotional reasoning can cause a racing heart or difficulty concentrating.

Tips:
1. **Gather Evidence:**
   Ask yourself the following questions:
   - What evidence do I have that supports this thought?
   - Is there any evidence that contradicts it?
   - Is there a more balanced way to think about this situation?
   - How would I advise a friend if they were feeling this way?
2. **Reframe Thoughts:** Instead of thinking, "I'm terrible at this," try, "I'm still learning and improving my skills."

3. **Look for Alternative Explanations:** For instance, if you feel like nobody likes you, consider that people might be busy or preoccupied with their lives. This can help you see that your feelings may not reflect reality.
4. **Breathing Exercises:** Focus on yourself for a few minutes. Inhale slowly through your nose. Hold your breath for a few seconds. Then, exhale slowly through your mouth. This helps calm your mind and allows you to observe your thoughts.
5. **Body Scanning:** Find a comfortable place to Lie down. Mentally scan your body from head to toe. Pay attention to different parts of your body and acknowledge how they feel. This can help you connect with your physical sensations and reduce anxiety.
6. **Mindful Observation:** Observe something in your environment closely. Notice its colors, shapes, and textures. This practice can help you focus your mind away from your distress and bring you back to the present moment.
7. **Journaling:** Write down your thoughts and feelings daily. Doing so can provide clarity and help you process your emotions more effectively.
8. **Use Positive Affirmations:**
    Examples:
    - "I am capable of overcoming challenges."
    - "My feelings do not define my reality."
    - "I have the skills and knowledge to succeed."
9. **Focus on Problem-Solving:** Identify the issue at hand. Brainstorm possible solutions.
    Questions to consider include:
    - What can I do to improve this situation?
    - Are there any steps I can take to alleviate my anxiety or stress?
    - How can I prepare myself for potential challenges?
10. **Self-Reflection:** Take time each day to ask yourself questions.
    Examples:
    - What emotions did I feel today?
    - What triggered those emotions?
    - How did I respond to those emotions?
11. **Seek Support:** Expressing feelings can lighten the emotional burden and lead to constructive feedback. Therapists and counselors can help you develop healthier thought patterns and coping strategies.

Your emotions are valid, but they do not always represent reality. Changing our thinking takes practice and patience, but the benefits are worth the effort.

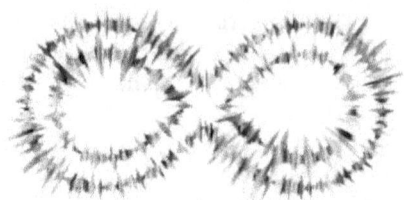

Should, Ought, Must Statements

Statements with "should," "ought," and "must" express what we believe we are obligated to do based on internal or external expectations. These words carry a sense of moral duty. For example, saying, "I should always get straight A's," sets a high standard for academic achievement.

While goals can be motivating, these statements can create feelings of pressure, guilt, or inadequacy when we don't meet them. When we tell ourselves, "I ought to help others before myself," we prioritize external expectations over our needs.

While altruism is commendable, excessive use of these statements can lead to self-neglect and burnout. Striking a balance between personal well-being and responsibilities is necessary for our health.

Saying, "I must be perfect in everything I do," can lead to fear of failure and perfectionism. As a result, we may avoid risks or challenges out of fear of failing.

Impact:
- **Increased Anxiety:** The belief that we must meet specific standards can create worry and fear about failure.
- **Low Self-Esteem:** If we don't meet our expectations, we may begin to feel like we are not good enough.
- **Procrastination:** Feeling overwhelmed by what we "should" do can sometimes lead to putting off tasks entirely.
- **Negative Self-Talk:** Using these statements can lead to harsh criticism of ourselves, making it hard to feel positive.

Aaron T. Beck introduced should, must, and ought statements in the 1960s. Instead of using rigid and demanding language, we can utilize strategies to overcome it.

Should, Ought, Must Statements

Tips:
1. **Challenge Your Thoughts:** For instance, if you think, "I should be better at math," consider whether this is true. Everyone learns at their own pace. It's okay to struggle with certain subjects. Recognizing that these thoughts may not be accurate can help reduce their power.
2. **Reframe Your Thoughts:** Instead of saying, "I should exercise," you can say, "I would like to exercise." This shift changes the obligation into a choice, making it feel less burdensome and more empowering.
3. **Use "Could" Instead:** For example, rather than saying, "I must finish all of my tasks," try "I could finish at least one of my objectives today." This change introduces flexibility toward possibilities rather than forcing a single outcome.
4. **Practice Self-Compassion:** Instead of saying, "I must get everything right," remind yourself that it's okay to make mistakes. You can say, "I will try my best, and it's okay if I don't get everything perfect." This mindset encourages growth and learning rather than fear of failure.
5. **Set Realistic Goals:** Rather than saying, "I ought to exercise every day," consider, "I can aim to exercise three times a week for 20 minutes each day." Setting a challenging yet attainable goal can help build confidence and motivation. This approach can motivate you without the weight of unrealistic expectations.
6. **Focus on the Present:** "Should," "ought," and "must" statements often draw our attention to the past or the future, leading to unnecessary stress. Focusing on the present moment reduces anxiety. Utilize deep breathing or meditation to help center your thoughts.
7. **Concentrate on What You Can Control:** Instead of saying, "I should be more organized," think, "I can work on organizing my study space this weekend." This approach empowers you to take action in a positive way.
8. **Use Positive Affirmations:** Rather than thinking, "I must always be successful," say, "I am learning and growing, and success comes in many forms." Positive affirmations can help reshape your mindset and encourage a more nurturing inner dialogue.
9. **Journal Your Thoughts:** When you notice "should," "ought," or "must" statements, write them down and then reframe them into more positive and realistic phrases. This practice can help you become aware of your patterns so you can change them over time.
10. **Seek Support:** Sharing your feelings can reduce feelings of pressure and alienation.

Giving ourselves kindness and understanding while working on our goals is worthwhile. Everyone struggles with these thoughts at times. Let's embrace the potential for positive communication by transforming rigid expectations into flexible possibilities. You can create a more supportive and encouraging inner dialogue with time and effort.

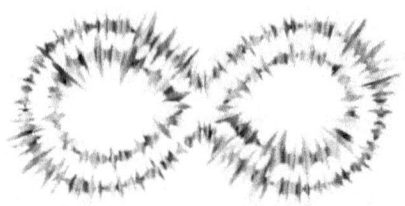

Comparison

The comparison trap is where individuals measure themselves against others. The credit for introducing the concept of comparison in psychology is often attributed to Wilhelm Wundt. He's a German psychologist widely regarded as the founder of experimental psychology in the late 19th century.

Wundt explored how individuals compare and contrast sensory experiences, such as colors, shapes, and sounds, to form complex perceptions of the world. This thinking often leads to feelings of inadequacy, jealousy, and low self-esteem.

This misrepresentation can lead to feelings of dissatisfaction with ourselves and our accomplishments. We may feel like we are never good enough. As a result, our internal dialogue becomes filled with competition and criticism, which erodes our confidence and worth.

Instead of focusing on our strengths and goals, we become preoccupied with comparing ourselves to others. This can lead to feeling superior or inferior. It can also create a sense of insecurity and self-doubt, making it difficult to assert our needs and boundaries.

A superiority complex stems from viewing oneself as inherently better in some way. It often arises from a deep-seated need for validation or a desire to feel more important than those around us. This mindset can be harmful because it fosters arrogance and a lack of empathy towards those perceived as inferior, which hinders genuine connections and mutual respect among peers.

An inferiority complex often arises when individuals perceive themselves as lacking compared to others. Whether it's comparing material possessions, achievements, or physical appearance, constantly viewing oneself as inferior to others can damage one's mental well-being.

Tips:
1. **Focus on Your Journey:** Everyone has different strengths, weaknesses, and paths to success. True self-worth comes from accepting oneself and embracing individual differences rather than constant comparison to others.

- **Set Personal Goals:** Write down your short-term and long-term goals. For instance, set a specific target, like raising your math grade by one letter.
- **Celebrate Small Victories:** Acknowledge your accomplishments, no matter how small. This practice helps shift your attention from others to your growth.

2. **Practice Gratitude:** Being thankful shifts your mindset from lack to abundance.
   - **Keep a Journal:** Write down three things you are grateful for daily. These can be simple, like a supportive friend or a good meal.
   - **Express Appreciation to Others:** Letting others know you appreciate them can strengthen relationships.
3. **Limit Social Media Exposure:** People often share only their best moments.
   - **Set Boundaries:** Decide specific times to check social platforms during the day. For example, only check it for 30 minutes after work.
   - **Curate Your Feed:** Follow accounts that uplift you. Unfollow accounts that make you feel inadequate or unhappy.
4. **Challenge Negative Thoughts:** Ask yourself if your comparison is based on facts.
5. **Reframe Your Thoughts:** Instead of thinking, "I will never be as good as them," try saying, "I am improving every day in my own way."
6. **Use Affirmations:** Phrases like "I am enough" or "I am capable of achieving my objectives" can help counteract negative self-talk.
7. **Cultivate Self-Compassion:** Acknowledge your feelings and reassure yourself that struggling is okay.
8. **Surround Yourself with Positive Influences:** Seek friends and mentors who uplift and encourage you. Positive influences can help you focus on your strengths rather than comparing yourself to others. Engaging in supportive communities through clubs, sports, or online groups can foster a sense of belonging and reduce the urge to compare.
9. **Seek Support:** Engage in open conversations with counselors or therapists. They can help you explore underlying issues contributing to these feelings and assist you in developing coping strategies.

There is no "one-size-fits-all" approach to success. Valuing ourselves for who we are rather than how we measure up to others fosters a more positive inner dialogue.

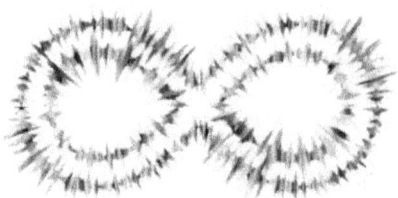

Personalization

Personalization involves attributing personal responsibility to things that are beyond our control. It includes when there is little evidence to support this belief and even when we are not at fault. When we consistently blame ourselves for every unfortunate circumstance, it can lead to intense feelings of guilt, shame, and inadequacy.

Fritz Heider is a prominent psychologist known for his contributions to social perception and attribution theory. In 1944, he conducted a famous experiment that illuminated the concept of personalization.

If someone performs poorly at something, they may immediately assume they are "stupid" or "not good enough." Fortunately, there are beneficial strategies that individuals can utilize to overcome personalization.

Tips:
1. **Challenge Negative Thoughts:** Learn to differentiate between feelings and reality. This strategy helps reduce the emotional weight of personalization and encourages a more rational approach to situations. When a person finds themselves thinking something like, "I must have done something wrong," they can ask questions like:
   - Was there something I could have controlled?
   - Am I considering all perspectives?
   - How would I advise someone else in this situation?
2. **Acknowledge Feelings:** Recognize that it's okay to feel upset or anxious. These feelings are natural.
3. **Talk to Yourself Kindly:** For example, say, "It's okay that I made a mistake; I can learn from this."
4. **Understand Shared Humanity:** Everyone makes mistakes and faces challenges. You are not alone in your experiences.
5. **Focus on the Facts:** Gather objective information about what is happening rather than jumping to conclusions. For example, if a friend is distant, instead of thinking, "They must not like me," consider other possibilities:
   - They might be going through a tough time.
   - They could be busy with other commitments.

6. **Focus on What You Can Control:** Concentrate on actionable steps rather than dwelling on past mistakes. Empower yourself to make positive changes without the burden of unnecessary guilt.
7. **Engage in Mindfulness Practices:** Techniques such as meditation, deep breathing, or yoga can help manage emotions and create a sense of calm.
8. **Keep a Journal:** After a while, you may notice recurring themes in which you blame yourself for things beyond your control.
9. **Use Positive Affirmations:** Repeat phrases like, "I am not responsible for others' feelings" or "I am doing my best."
10. **Seek Feedback and Support:** Support groups or counseling can be beneficial. Discussing feelings about a situation might reveal that others felt similarly.

Understand that you are not solely responsible for every disadvantageous event that occurs. Releasing unnecessary stress is liberating.

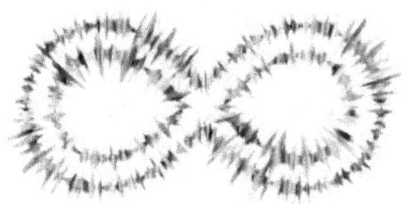

Blaming

Blaming attributes the cause of problems to external factors. Accusing others prevents the accuser from taking responsibility for their actions. A pioneering figure in social psychology named Fritz Heider introduced the concept of attribution theory. It explores how individuals interpret and explain their behavior and those of others.

In 1958, Heider's work laid the foundation for understanding how people attribute the causes of events. He proposed that individuals attribute behavior to internal dispositions, such as personality traits, or external circumstances, such as situational factors.

When someone blames others, they point fingers at others instead of engaging in constructive dialogue. This can create a hostile environment where individuals feel attacked and defensive, making it strenuous to have productive conversations.

Refusing to accept responsibility for actions can erode trust in relationships. Without accountability, communication breaks down due to a lack of honesty and transparency.

As one person blames another, the accused individual may become defensive and retaliate by placing blame back. This back-and-forth cycle escalates tensions and prevents any meaningful resolution from taking place. Ultimately, both parties may feel unheard and resentful, further damaging their communication.

Tips:
1. **Practice Self-Reflection:** Take time to think about your thoughts, feelings, and actions. Here are some steps to practice reflection:
    - **Set Aside Quiet Time:** Find a comfortable space to think without distractions. This could be in your room, in a quiet park, or even during a walk.
    - **Journal Your Thoughts:** Clear your mind by writing down your thoughts and feelings. You might start with, "I felt upset when..." and continue to explore why you felt that way.
    - **Identify Triggers:** Look for patterns in your thoughts. Do you tend to blame others in specific situations? Recognizing triggers can help you prepare for them in the future.

- **Ask Questions:** Dig deeper into your feelings. For example, if you blame a friend for not inviting you to an event, ask yourself what bothers you. Is it about feeling left out, or is it about feeling unvalued?
2. **Acknowledge Your Feelings:** If you feel upset about a situation, take a moment to identify your emotions. Are you angry, sad, or frustrated? Write down your feelings in a journal to help clarify your thoughts.
3. **Shift Your Perspective:** Instead of viewing a situation as someone else's fault, see it from different angles. Ask yourself, "What could I have done differently?" or "What can I learn from this experience?"
4. **Alter Your Language:** Communicate openly while utilizing the following bullet points.
    - **Use "I" Statements:** Rather than saying, "You made me feel bad," rephrase it to, "I felt bad when that happened."
    - **Avoid Absolutes:** Words like "always" and "never" can exaggerate the situation and lead to blaming. Instead of saying, "You never listen to me," try, "I feel unheard when we don't discuss things."
    - **Acknowledge Your Role:** Use language that recognizes your contribution to situations. Instead of saying, "It's your fault I'm upset," say, "I realized I may have misunderstood what you meant."
5. **Practice Mindfulness:** Deep breathing or meditation can help you manage your emotions and reduce the urge to blame.
6. **Develop Empathy:** The following bullet points can enhance your empathetic skills.
    - **Listen Actively:** Concentrate on understanding what the speaker intends to convey.
    - **Practice Compassion:** Consider the other person's feelings and circumstances. For example, "Maybe they were having a tough day too."
    - **Engage in Perspective-Taking:** Imagine how the other person feels. This can help you realize that, like you, they have their struggles and reasons for their actions.
7. **Identify Areas for Improvement:** Think about situations where you tend to blame others. What role did you play in this conflict? What skills could you develop to handle these situations better?
8. **Create Smart Goals:** For example, "I will study for 30 minutes each day to prepare for my next test."
9. **Celebrate Progress:** Acknowledge your achievements to encourage you to continue working on your goals.
10. **Focus on Solutions:** Ask yourself, "What can I do to improve this situation?" This proactive approach empowers you while encouraging teamwork and collaboration. For example, if a group project fails, instead of blaming a teammate, discuss what went wrong and how everyone can contribute to improving it next time.

11. **Seek Support:** Asking for help doesn't mean you are weak. Being willing to learn and grow takes strength.

We all have accountability in every situation. Everyone makes mistakes. It's how we respond that truly matters. Every step you take toward personal responsibility is a step toward growth.

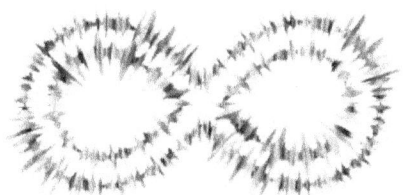

Jumping to Conclusions

Jumping to conclusions means making negative interpretations without any concrete evidence. For example, assuming we know what others think about us may create self-doubt and insecurity. Similarly, predicting gloomy outcomes without evidence can lead to self-sabotage and anxiety.

Dr. Daniel Kahneman is a renowned psychologist and Nobel laureate who studied the concept of jumping to conclusions. Through experiments in the 1970s and 1980s, Dr. Kahneman and his colleague, Dr. Amos Tversky, demonstrated how people often rely on mental shortcuts when making judgments and decisions.

When we engage in this thinking, we create a false narrative that distorts our self-perception. For instance, if we automatically assume that we will fail a task without trying, we limit our potential for success. This can become a self-fulfilling prophecy reinforcing our belief in our perceived shortcomings.

Prematurely overlooking alternative perspectives and solutions can have dangerous consequences in our personal and professional lives. For example, if we assume that our boss is angry with us because they didn't say hello this morning, we might start avoiding them, which could harm our working relationship.

Tips:
1. **Recognize the Signs:** Pay attention to your thoughts and feelings. Do you often think the worst when something goes wrong? Do you assume that others judge you or think negatively about your actions?

    Imagine you see your friend talking to someone else in the lunchroom. You might think, "They must be mad at me, or they don't want to be friends anymore." Recognizing that this thought is based on limited information can help you pause and reassess the situation.
2. **Challenge Your Thoughts:** If you need clarification, ask questions to get more information. You can do this directly or indirectly.
    - What caused this thought?

- Could there be another explanation for what I'm experiencing?
- What would I tell a friend if they were in my situation?

If you think, "I failed that test, so I'm not smart," challenge that thought by considering your past successes. Have you done well at anything before? Did you study enough for this test? Recognizing the difference between a single test result and your overall ability can help avoid skewed conclusions.

3. **Use Concrete Evidence:** What do I know? What can I find out?
4. **Consider Other Perspectives:** Think about how others view the situation. What might they be thinking or feeling?
5. **Acknowledge Your Feelings:** It's okay to feel upset or anxious. Everyone has moments of doubt.
6. **Speak to Yourself Positively:** Instead of saying, "I'm such a failure," try, "I made a mistake, but I can learn from it."
7. **Practice Mindfulness:**
    - **Deep Breathing:** Calm your mind and body by taking deep breaths. This can help clear your thoughts and reduce anxiety.
    - **Focus on the Present:** Keep your attention on what is going on right now rather than worrying about what might happen in the future.
    - **Observe Your Thoughts:** Instead of reacting to your thoughts, observe them without judgment. This can help you understand them better.
8. **Focus on the Present:**
    - **Observe Your Surroundings:** Notice what you can see, hear, and feel. This practice can reduce anxiety.
    - **Active Engagement:** Participate in activities you enjoy.
9. **Seek Support:** Engage with others who can provide a supportive environment for discussing your thoughts and feelings. Ask a mentor. Join a group or club.

It's imperative to step back and reassess a situation before concluding. With practice, you can improve your overall well-being.

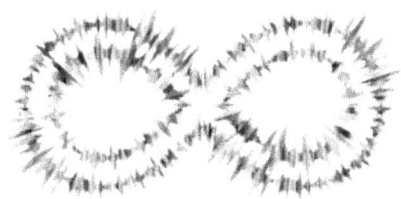

Mind Reading

Mind reading occurs when someone believes they know what others think, even when no concrete evidence supports this belief. For example, convincing ourselves that others are judging or criticizing us can lead to negative self-talk and feelings of inadequacy.

The exploration of mind reading can be traced back to the late 19th century when a pioneering psychologist named William James delved into the study of consciousness and mental processes. He is often praised as the "Father of American Psychology." He was intrigued by the idea of understanding how individuals perceive and interpret the thoughts of others without any external cues.

When we engage in mind reading, we project our insecurities. This can hinder our personal development because we cannot accurately assess our strengths and weaknesses.

Assuming we know what others think about us may cause us to withdraw from social interactions and relationships. This presumption can create a vicious cycle in which our distorted beliefs about ourselves prevent us from forming meaningful connections with others.

Impact:
- **Miscommunication:** Assuming what others think can lead to incorrect conclusions. This might cause conflicts or feelings of isolation.
- **Distress:** Constantly worrying about others' opinions can increase stress and anxiety.
- **Self-Esteem:** If we believe others think poorly of us, it can harm our confidence.

Tips:
1. **Recognize When It Happens:** Often, these thoughts can occur automatically and may feel like facts. Pay attention to your thoughts throughout the day. Ask yourself questions such as:
    - What evidence do I have for this thought?
    - Am I jumping to conclusions?
    - Could there be another explanation for this situation?

2. **Keep a Journal:** Track your thoughts and feelings. Write down situations where you felt you were mind reading and reflect on the outcomes.
3. **Challenge Your Thoughts:** We tend to guess what others think based on our feelings or limited understanding. Utilize the following techniques to help you challenge these thoughts.
   - **Ask for Clarification:** Instead of assuming what someone is thinking, it's better to ask them directly. A simple "Hey, I noticed you've been quiet lately. What's on your mind?" can clear up misunderstandings.
   - **Consider Alternative Explanations:** For example, if someone doesn't say hi to you, they might be lost in thought or have not seen you.
   - **Look for Evidence:** If you think someone is annoyed with you, remember times when they complimented you or showed interest in your progress.
4. **Acknowledge Your Feelings:** Everyone makes mistakes. Ask yourself what caused you to feel hurt or worried when you think someone is upset with you.
5. **Talk to Yourself Positively:** Instead of saying, "They are mad at me," try, "We are doing the best we can at the moment."
6. **Engage in Relaxation Techniques:** Mindfulness, deep breathing, or meditation can help you calm your mind and focus on the present moment.
7. **Focus on Facts, Not Feelings:** For example, instead of thinking, "They must think I'm not trying," consider what you know. Have they given you any feedback? Have you completed your tasks? Ground yourself in facts to help you see the situation more clearly.
8. **Limit Overthinking:** When you find yourself stuck in a cycle of negative thoughts, limit your time on them. Set a timer for five minutes to think about the situation. After that, distract yourself with a different activity that interests you. You will break the overthinking cycle, allowing you to return to the problem with a fresh perspective.
9. **Develop Healthy Communication Skills:** Practice being open and honest with others. Share your thoughts and feelings without assuming you know theirs. Encourage them to do the same. This two-way communication helps build trust and understanding in relationships.
10. **Listen Actively:** When someone speaks to you, focus entirely on what they say. This helps you better understand their perspective rather than thinking about your response.
11. **Spend Quality Time Together:** You will better understand situations. Engage in activities you both enjoy to encourage a deeper connection.

12. **Seek Help:** If you find that thoughts are negatively impacting your life and relationships, consider seeking help from a mental health professional. Therapists can provide you with additional strategies and support to address cognitive distortions. Cognitive-behavioral therapy (CBT) is an effective tool for challenging and changing negative thought patterns.

Clear and open communication is the key to better understanding ourselves and others. Take the necessary time to practice changing your thinking.

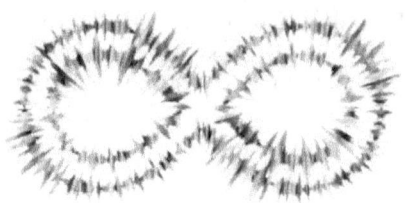

Fortune Telling

Fortune telling predicts outcomes for future events without any concrete evidence to support them. In psychology, fortune telling is often associated with the "Barnum effect." One of the pioneers in recognizing the connection between fortune telling and psychology was the American psychologist Bertram Forer. In the 1940s, Forer conducted a famous experiment demonstrating how individuals accept vague and general personality descriptions as highly accurate.

When individuals engage in fortune telling, they often imagine the worst-case scenarios and convince themselves that these scenarios are inevitable. This pessimistic outlook can lead to self-doubt, anxiety, and fear, which can affect their confidence and self-esteem. For instance, someone may believe they will fail a job interview before even trying, leading to feelings of inadequacy and reluctance to make an effort effectively.

Individuals may avoid sharing their thoughts and feelings with others because they assume their ideas will be rejected or criticized. This prediction can lead to feelings of isolation and loneliness.

When individuals constantly anticipate unfortunate outcomes, they may avoid taking risks or trying new experiences. This can limit personal growth and prevent individuals from reaching their full potential. For instance, someone may decline a leadership opportunity because they predict failure. It causes them to miss valuable learning experiences and personal development.

The beliefs and emotions associated with this distortion influence how individuals perceive and respond to communication from others. For example, someone who believes they are unlikable may misinterpret compliments or positive feedback.

Tips:
1. **Challenge Negative Predictions:**
   Ask yourself the following questions.
   - What evidence do I have for this prediction? Is there concrete information supporting my belief that something terrible will happen?

- Have I ever predicted something negative that didn't come true? Reflecting on past experiences can help you see that many of your fears may be unfounded.
- What is the worst that could happen, and how would I handle it? Sometimes, thinking through the worst-case scenario can help you realize you have the skills to cope with challenges.

Often, you'll find that there is little to no evidence to back up your fears. For instance, if you think, "I will fail my math test," try to recall cases in which you prepared well and did succeed. Keep a record of your achievements to help counter this thinking.

2. **Reframe Your Thoughts**: Instead of, "I will mess up my presentation," try saying, "I am prepared, and I will do my best." Write these affirmations down and read them daily to help shift your mindset over time.
3. **Reality Check:** If you think, "Everyone will laugh at me," consider times when people have supported you or been kind. Gathering evidence can help you see that your predictions may be exaggerated.
4. **Concentrate on the Present:**
    - **Deep Breathing:** Take slow breaths to calm your mind and body. Focus on how your breath enters and leaves your lungs.
    - **Grounding Techniques:** Use your senses to bring yourself to the present. What do you see, hear, smell, or feel right now? Doing so can distract you from anxious thoughts about the future.
    - **Journaling:** Process your emotions by writing them down.
5. **Practice Self-Compassion:** It's okay to have fears. How we manage them is what matters.
6. **Set Realistic Goals:** Instead of saying, "I want to do better in school," try, "I will study for 30 minutes every day after school." Specific goals are easier to follow. Record your progress. Give yourself a deadline.
7. **Talk About Your Feelings:** Sharing your thoughts with someone you trust can relieve stress and provide new perspectives. They may help you see that your predictions are less likely than you think.
8. **Join a Support Group:** Many schools or communities have groups focused on mental health.
9. **Consider Professional Help:** If fortune telling significantly impacts your life, speaking with a counselor or therapist can be very helpful. They can provide coping strategies tailored to your needs.

It is possible to improve your mental well-being by changing how you think. Each step you take leads to greater confidence and enhanced self-communication.

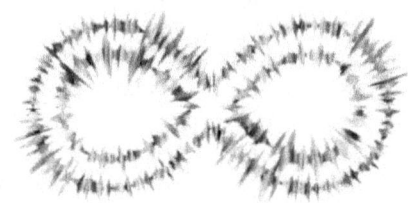

Always Being Right

The "always being right syndrome" stubbornly holds onto beliefs without considering alternative perspectives or being open to feedback. When a person falls into the trap of always being right, they tend to dismiss contradictory evidence or opinions that challenge their viewpoint.

This can lead to a sense of superiority, defensiveness, and an unwillingness to consider other valid viewpoints. The individual believes their way of thinking is the only correct way, which shuts down opportunities for growth, learning, and effective communication.

In the 1950s, psychologist Leon Festinger developed the theory of cognitive dissonance, which analyzes the discomfort individuals feel when faced with conflicting beliefs and behaviors. Cognitive dissonance is closely related to always being right because it highlights how people strive to maintain consistency in their beliefs and actions, even if it means ignoring contradictory information.

One famous example of the concept of always being right is groupthink, where individuals within a group prioritize consensus and harmony over critical evaluation of different ideas. This can lead to flawed decision-making processes and a lack of innovation within the group. Social media platforms perpetuate this thinking because individuals are exposed primarily to data that aligns with their existing beliefs.

Insisting on infallibility hinders introspection, awareness, and personal growth. This thinking can manifest in various ways.

Common Signs:
- **Closed-Mindedness:** Individuals who always believe they are right may dismiss new ideas, feedback, or self-reflection. This blockage can hinder their ability to gain insight into their thoughts or emotions.
- **Inner Turmoil:** When faced with facts that counter their beliefs, individuals may experience cognitive dissonance. This inconsistency can lead to stress, anxiety, and a sense of being 'stuck' in one's perspective.

- **Lack of Growth:** Refusing to acknowledge and learn from mistakes traps individuals in the cycle of always being right, stunting their personal and interpersonal growth. Personal development often requires humility, openness to feedback, and a willingness to challenge one's beliefs or assumptions.

Impact:
- **Strained Relationships:** When individuals insist on being right, it can create tension in relationships. Being unwilling to consider alternative ideas or approaches can cause misunderstanding. Friends, family members, and classmates may feel dismissed or invalidated.
- **Self-Criticism:** People who believe they must always be right may judge themselves harshly for mistakes.
- **Resistance to Growth:** The mindset of always needing to be right can hinder personal growth. It can prevent them from developing critical thinking skills and emotional intelligence.

Tips:
1. **Practice Active Listening:** Try to understand different viewpoints without immediately jumping to defend your perspective. No one is exact in their comprehension.
   - **Prioritize the Speaker:** Avoid distractions like phones or computers and make eye contact with the person speaking.
   - **Show Understanding:** Nod or use verbal affirmations like "I see" or "I understand" to show that you are engaged.
   - **Reflect:** Paraphrase the speaker's words to ensure you understand their point of view. For example, you might say, "So what you're saying is..."
   - **Ask Clarification Questions:** If something is unclear, ask questions to clarify. This shows that you value their opinion and want to understand better.
2. **Ask Yourself:** Why do I feel the need to be right in this situation? What are the consequences of insisting on being right? How might my perspective affect my relationships?
3. **Use Positive Self-Talk:**
   - "It's okay to be wrong sometimes because I can learn from it."
   - "I value my perspective, but I am also open to others."
   - "Learning is more important than being right."
4. **Set Learning Goals:** Instead of aiming to be correct, set goals to learn and improve. For example, aim to understand a topic better rather than simply getting the correct answer.
5. **Celebrate Effort:** Acknowledge your hard work and effort, even when the outcome isn't perfect. This recognition can help you appreciate the learning process.

6. **Embrace Errors as Learning Opportunities:**
    - **Acknowledge Your Mistakes:** When you make a mistake, admit it. This can be difficult, but it is vital to personal growth.
    - **Reflect on What Went Wrong:** Take time to think about what led to the mistake. What could you have done differently?
    - **Receive Feedback:** Ask others for their input on the situation. This can provide new insights and help you improve in the future.
    - **Set Goals for Improvement:** Create specific goals to help you avoid making the same mistake again. This can boost your confidence and encourage a growth mindset.
    - **Challenge Your Assumptions:** Regularly challenge your assumptions and beliefs. Ask yourself why you hold certain beliefs and whether they are based on evidence or personal biases.
    - **Reframe Your Thinking:** Reduce any fear of being wrong. Instead of thinking, "I was wrong," try saying, "I have learned something new."
    - **Share Your Mistakes:** Talking about your mistakes with friends or family can help normalize the experience. This openness can strengthen relationships and create a supportive environment.
7. **Cultivate Empathy:** Embrace humility by acknowledging that you are fallible and that it is okay to be wrong sometimes. Recognizing that human errors occur and learning from them is a natural part of personal growth.
    - **Put Yourself in Others' Shoes:** Imagine how others feel about a situation. Consider their experiences and emotions when discussing differing opinions.
    - **Practice Kindness:** Show kindness and understanding when others express their viewpoints. This creates a safe space for open dialogue.
    - **Engage in Diverse Conversations:** Broaden your understanding and appreciation of varied opinions. Talk to people from different backgrounds and perspectives.
    - **Be Open to Change:** Recognize that your viewpoint may not always be the best.
8. **Collaborate:** When working with others, prioritize teamwork over individual success. Here are some tips for fostering collaboration:
    - **Encourage Group Input:** Create a sense of shared ownership and responsibility by inviting everyone to share their thoughts and ideas.
    - **Value Different Opinions:** Diverse perspectives can lead to better solutions. Celebrate the strengths each team member brings to the table.

- **Create a Supportive Environment:** Discuss opinions compassionately. This can lead to more productive conversations.
- **Concentrate on Common Goals:** Keep the group's objectives in mind. This can help shift the focus away from individual validation to collective success.

9. **Explore Other Perspectives:**
   - **Focus on the Speaker:** Pay full attention to the person speaking without planning your response while they are talking.
   - **Ask Questions:** Show interest in the other person's viewpoint by asking clarifying questions. This demonstrates that you value their opinion.
   - **Summarize What You Heard:** Repeat the speaker's words to ensure you understand their perspective correctly. This technique can help foster open communication.

Everyone makes inaccuracies. Learning from our experiences is what truly matters. Instead of fearing mistakes, try to view them as opportunities for growth.

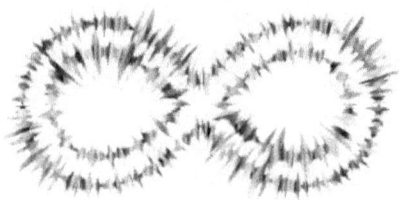

The Truth Behind Illusions

Perception refers to the way we make sense of the world around us. It involves using our senses, experiences, and beliefs to understand what is happening. What we interpret is not always an accurate representation of reality. Our minds can play tricks on us by leading us to believe things that may not be true. This disconnect between perception and reality is a fascinating feature of human cognition that can be observed in various situations.

One striking example of how perception can deceive us is through optical illusions. These mind-bending images are like puzzles for our brains, tricking us into seeing something that isn't there. They exploit the way our brains process visual information, causing us to perceive depth, motion, or color inaccurately.

Take the famous "Rubin vase" illusion, for instance. It presents an image that can be discerned as either a vase or two faces in profile, reliant upon how our brain processes the information.

Past experiences, biases, assumptions, and external sources of information can easily influence our minds. These preconceived notions can distort the way we see the world, leading us to misinterpret events or people.

For example, if an individual has had unfavorable encounters with dogs, they may perceive all dogs as threatening even if they pose no actual danger. This distortion of reality based on past experiences demonstrates how perception can differ from reality.

In today's era, we are continuously engulfed with information and images that may not always reflect the truth. Filters, editing, and selective sharing on social media platforms can create a distorted view of people's lives by making them appear happier, more successful, or more attractive than they are. This superimposed rendition of reality can lead to feelings of imperfection and fear of missing out among viewers who compare themselves to these idealized representations.

Things are not always as they appear. Acknowledging the limitations of our perception empowers us to see the world more objectively and critically evaluate the information presented to us. Look beyond the surface to uncover the truth beneath illusions.

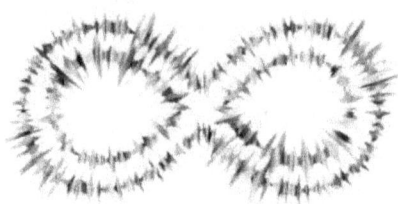

Acknowledging Denial

Denial is a common defense mechanism that many people use to cope with challenging situations or emotions. When someone is in denial, they often refuse to accept the reality of a condition because it is too painful or overwhelming to acknowledge. While denial may provide temporary relief, it can significantly impact the ability to communicate effectively with oneself.

Sigmund Freud introduced the concept of denial in the late 19th century. He's a famous Austrian neurologist and psychoanalyst. His work on denial stemmed from his groundbreaking studies on defense mechanisms. The mind develops these strategies to protect itself from distress.

According to Freud, denial is a way for individuals to avoid facing uncomfortable truths about themselves or their circumstances. Denying the existence of a dilemma tricks people into temporarily alleviating their anxiety. This deception causes them to believe they are maintaining a sense of psychological equilibrium.

Fear is a compelling emotion that can often lead to denial as a defense mechanism. For instance, a person who is afraid of public speaking may refuse opportunities to speak in public, convincing themselves that they are not interested or capable despite the potential benefits.

Denial enables people to avoid addressing the source of their fear by temporarily creating a false sense of security. Denying the existence of something frightening or challenging hinders their ability to confront or overcome their fears in the long run.

Fear of rejection can often trigger denial as a defense mechanism to shield oneself from anticipated emotional pain. Rejecting this possibility before it occurs permits individuals to shield themselves from the perceived threat to their self-esteem and sense of belonging.

When individuals deny certain aspects of themselves or their experiences, they may avoid accurately reflecting on their thoughts, feelings, and behaviors. This lack of self-awareness can prevent them from understanding the root causes of their emotions or behaviors, leading to misunderstandings and conflicts with themselves and others.

This distorted perception of reality makes seeing things as they are challenging. It can cloud judgment and inhibit critical thinking. As a result, individuals in denial may struggle to address their internal struggles or communicate effectively with themselves about their needs and desires.

Avoiding uncomfortable truths may cause individuals to depend on unhealthy coping mechanisms such as avoidance, suppression, or numbing. These maladaptive strategies can prevent individuals from processing their emotions constructively.

Ignoring authentic thoughts and feelings undermines integrity, leading to feelings of insecurity, self-doubt, or internal conflict.

Tips:
1. **Acknowledge Your Feelings:** This means being honest with yourself about what you are experiencing. Write your experiences in a journal to explore your emotions.
2. **Educate Yourself:** Sometimes, denial stems from a lack of understanding. Educating yourself about your situation can empower you to confront brutal truths. For example, if you are struggling with an addiction, reading about the effects of substance abuse can help you recognize the need for change.
3. **Set Realistic Goals:** Start with small steps toward acceptance. For instance, if you are in denial about your health, you might set a goal to exercise for 15 minutes a day. These small victories can build your confidence and motivate you to face larger challenges.
4. **Practice Mindfulness:** Focus on the present moment in a safe space to reduce anxiety. Engage in meditation or deep breathing techniques to help you stay grounded.
5. **Challenge Negative Thoughts:** Ask yourself, "Is this thought based on reality?" or "What evidence do I have to support this belief?"
6. **Embrace Change:** Recognize that life is constantly evolving. Instead of resisting change, try to view it as an opportunity for growth. Accepting that change is inevitable can help you move past denial and adapt to new circumstances.
7. **Seek Help:** While it's natural to experience denial from time to time, there are instances where talking to a qualified mental health practitioner is critical for overcoming this defense mechanism. Some situations in which professional support may be beneficial include:
    - **Persistent Feelings of Discomfort:** An individual who consistently feels anxious, stressed, or overwhelmed but chooses to ignore these emotions may signal that denial is at play.
    - **Impact on Relationships:** Communication can deteriorate due to avoidance of problematic topics.
    - **Physical Symptoms:** Sometimes, denial can manifest in physical symptoms like headaches, stomach issues, or muscle tension. If these symptoms persist despite medical evaluation, exploring the psychological factors contributing to them may be beneficial.

- **Unhealthy Coping Mechanisms:** Engaging in harmful behaviors like substance abuse, compulsive shopping, or disordered eating can be a sign of concealed matters that are being masked by denial. These behaviors harm physical health, strain relationships, and hinder personal growth.

Experienced mental health providers such as therapists, counselors, or psychologists are educated on assisting individuals with navigating through denial and other defense mechanisms. They provide a safe and supportive space for clients to explore internal and external behaviors.

Through therapy, individuals can:
- Gain awareness of their denial patterns and how they impact their life
- Explore underlying issues contributing to denial
- Strengthen their self-awareness and emotional resilience
- Expand on healthy coping strategies to manage difficult emotions

Denial is a common initial reaction when faced with unwanted or challenging situations. People might refuse to accept the reality of a concern because it feels too overwhelming or complicated to process.

Prolonged denial can lead to feelings of frustration and helplessness. When individuals deny their emotions or facts, they are more likely to experience heightened irritability.

It takes time and effort to overcome denial, but the rewards of acceptance are worth it. Facing the truth can lead to a healthier, more fulfilling life.

Addressing Anger

Emotions such as anger can significantly impact how we communicate with ourselves. Anger is a strong feeling of displeasure or hostility that arises when we feel threatened, mistreated, or frustrated. When we experience anger, it can influence our thoughts, perceptions, and self-talk.

One of the primary figures who uncovered the significance of anger in psychology was William James. In the late 19th century, James proposed the theory of emotion, which suggested that our feelings result from how we interpret our bodily sensations in response to different stimuli. He believed that emotions like anger play an alluring role in shaping our behavior and interactions with the world around us.

Unacknowledged concerns can lead to feelings of resentment. When our needs are not addressed, we can feel unheard. This lack of validation can build up over time, causing emotions to manifest as anger.

When we are angry, our ability to discern logically and consider alternative solutions is compromised. Harsh self-criticism over situations that are beyond our control may arise. This pessimistic self-talk can lead to shame, guilt, and low self-esteem.

Unresolved anger can seep into our interactions with others, damaging our relationships and hindering our social communication. When we struggle to manage our anger, we may lash out, become defensive, or withdraw from communication. These barriers can prevent us from forming meaningful connections and expressing ourselves authentically.

We may act impulsively, say things we later regret, or make hasty decisions without thoroughly evaluating the consequences. This can lead to further aggravation and conflicts.

When someone is consumed by anger, they can feel an overwhelming need to bring others down in an attempt to feel better about themselves. This behavior often stems from feelings of insecurity, powerlessness, or inadequacy, and putting others down can temporarily boost one's ego at the other person's expense.

This cycle of negativity destroys relationships. It also reinforces a harmful pattern of seeking validation by tearing others apart through negging, gaslighting, quick wit, or sarcasm.

Negging is a manipulative tactic where someone gives backhanded compliments or subtle insults to undermine another person's confidence. It often stems from deep-seated feelings of inadequacy. Understanding the roots of negging can help individuals address their underlying issues and choose more productive ways to navigate social interactions.

Gaslighting is a manipulative tactic where one person makes another person question their thoughts, feelings, and reality. This behavior often stems from deep-rooted feelings of anger within the gaslighter.

When individuals experience anger, they may seek to regain control by undermining others' confidence and perceptions. Gaslighters mask their underlying anger with psychological control techniques in an attempt to exert dominance over a situation or person. Phrases such as "It was just a joke" without apologizing may be used to invalidate someone.

Quick wit and sarcasm are often linked to anger because they can be used as defense mechanisms. When someone feels angry, they might use quick wit or sarcasm to deflect their genuine emotions as a way to protect themselves.

Making clever or sarcastic remarks enables them to release pent-up frustrations in a more socially conditioned manner. These destructive statements often stem from deeper emotions, such as unresolved anger, that need to be acknowledged and addressed. There are effective ways to express intelligence without being demeaning.

Most people dislike communication styles such as negging, gaslighting, sarcasm, and quick witted responses for various reasons. Consider when people expressing these tactics can dish it but can't take it. They may lash back by calling you judgey or blaming you for something to empower their ego in an attempt to regain control.

Signs that may suggest a need for professional intervention include:
- **Frequency and Intensity:** Consistent involvement in aggressive behavior or outbursts
- **Impact on Relationships:** Anger affects relationships with family, friends, or colleagues
- **Physical Symptoms:** Experiencing headaches, rapid heartbeat, or digestive issues suspected to be caused by anger
- **Difficulty in Managing Anger:** Struggling to control anger or finding that coping strategies are ineffective.
- **Negative Consequences:** When anger leads to negative consequences such as legal issues, job loss, or social isolation.

Tips:
1. **Recognize Triggers:** Everyone experiences triggers differently. Identify your triggers to help you prepare for situations that may provoke anger. Some common triggers include:
    - **Stress:** High levels of stress from school, work, or personal life
    - **Frustration:** Situations that do not go as planned

- **Feeling Ignored:** When people feel overlooked or unappreciated
- **Conflict with Others:** Disagreements or misunderstandings
2. **Keep a Journal:** Note when you feel angry and what caused it.
3. **Practice Deep Breathing:** When we become angry, our bodies go into a fight-or-flight response, leading to increased heart rate and tension. Here's how to calm your mind and body through deep breathing:
    - **Find a Quiet Space:** If possible, step away from the situation that makes you angry.
    - **Inhale Deeply:** Breathe in slowly through your nose for a count of four.
    - **Hold Your Breath:** Keep the air in your lungs for a count of four.
    - **Exhale Slowly:** Release the breath through your mouth for a count of four.
    - **Repeat:** Do this several times until you feel more relaxed.
4. **Use "I" Statements:** This approach can reduce defensiveness and promote understanding. For example:
    - Instead of saying, "You never listen to me," try, "I feel ignored when I'm not heard."
    - Instead of saying, "You made me angry," say, "I felt angry when that happened."
5. **Take a Break:** When emotions run high, it can be challenging to think clearly. Stepping away allows you to cool down and reflect on your feelings. Here are some ways to take a break:
    - **Go for a Walk:** Physical activity can help release built-up energy and reduce stress.
    - **Listen to Music:** This powerful tool can alter your mood and calm your mind.
    - **Engage in a Hobby:** Distracting yourself through a favorite activity can help shift your focus away from anger.
6. **Exercise Regularly:** 30 minutes of physical activity three days per week is a good baseline, whether walking, dancing, playing sports, or any other activity you enjoy. Intentional movement can help reduce stress and improve mood. Here are some ways exercise can help with anger management:
    - **Releases Endorphins:** Physical activity releases chemicals in the brain called endorphins. They can improve your mood and create a sense of happiness.
    - **Reduces Tension:** Exercise can help relieve muscle tension and reduce feelings of anger.
    - **Provides a Healthy Outlet:** Channeling your energy into exercise can be a healthy distraction from anger.

7. **Seek Support:** Consulting a mental health professional can be beneficial in various situations. The following information includes some scenarios where it may be appropriate to consult a qualified practitioner.
    - **Persistent Anger:** If feelings of anger persist over an extended period
    - **History of Trauma:** Individuals with a history of trauma or abusive experiences
    - **Difficulty in Communication:** When difficulties in expressing anger or conflicts arise
    - **Self-Harm or Destructive Behavior:** Engaging in self-harm, destructive behavior, or thoughts of harming others
    - **Underlying Mental Health Issues:** Underlying mental health concerns manifest as depression or anxiety

Anger is a personal truth that needs resolution. How you respond can make all the difference.

Unsettled Bargaining

Bargaining is the process of finding a resolution that satisfies desires. It was first introduced by psychiatrist Elisabeth Kübler-Ross in 1969. Someone may attempt to negotiate with a higher power or fate in an effort to postpone or prevent an inevitable loss. They may make promises or try to find ways to regain control over the situation.

When we bargain with ourselves, we weigh different options to find a solution that meets our needs. This internal negotiation can lead to conflicting thoughts and emotions as we reconcile competing priorities. For example, suppose we are trying to decide whether to study for an upcoming test or hang out with friends. In that case, we may experience inner turmoil as we strive to balance our academic responsibilities and social needs.

Constantly weighing options to reach a compromise within one's mind can create stress and confusion. It can result in a lack of confidence in one's choices and abilities.

Evaluating our worth, needs, and desires can either boost or diminish our self-esteem. For example, if we constantly bargain with ourselves over indulging in unhealthy foods, we may see ourselves as lacking willpower or self-control.

Evaluating different choices can sometimes lead to indecision or procrastination as we struggle to find the perfect solution. If we cannot decide in a timely manner, this internal negotiation can sometimes result in delays or missed opportunities.

Determining what is most important to us can affect our ability to pursue goals effectively. For example, if we constantly bargain with ourselves about exercising regularly, we may struggle to stay motivated and committed to our fitness.

Signs that someone may be experiencing bargaining:
- **Persistent Feelings of Guilt:** If an individual constantly believes that they are somehow responsible for situations they encounter
- **Avoidance of Reality:** A complete avoidance of accepting the reality of a situation can hinder the healing process
- **Interference with Daily Life:** Activities such as work, school, or relationships are negatively impacted

- **Persistent Anxiety or Depression:** Continuous feelings of anxiety, depression, or hopelessness

Tips:
1. **Set Clear Goals:** It is easier to stay committed when goals are specific, measurable, and realistic. For example, instead of saying, "I want to be fit," try setting a goal such as, "I will work on my fitness for 30 minutes three times a week."
2. **Create a Routine:** Establishing a routine provides structure, making it easier to follow through on tasks. For instance, if you allocate specific times for homework, exercise, and relaxation, you are less likely to convince yourself to skip a task.
3. **Practice Mindfulness:** Deep breathing, meditation, or simply pausing to assess your thoughts can create space for better decisions. For example, if you notice yourself bargaining about studying, take a moment to breathe deeply and reflect on your goals. This awareness can help you choose actions aligned with your values.
4. **Use Positive Self-Talk:** Instead of saying, "I deserve a break because I worked hard," try framing it positively: "I can reward myself with a break after I finish my homework." This approach reinforces the idea that completing tasks is beneficial and encourages commitment.
5. **Be Accountable:** Share your goals with people who will support you. When someone is aware of your commitments, you may feel less inclined to put them off.
6. **Reflect on Outcomes:** Keep a journal where you record your thoughts about decisions and their outcomes to help reinforce the habit of making better choices.
7. **Limit Choices:** Too many options can lead to indecisiveness. Limiting your choices can simplify decision-making so you can focus on what truly matters. For example, choose one or two activities you enjoy the most instead of deciding between multiple options.
8. **Seek Help:** The following bullet points include the benefits of receiving professional help.
   - **Validation of Emotions:** Individuals can confidentially disclose their feelings, which helps them feel understood and supported.
   - **Developing Coping Skills:** Professionals can advise individuals about healthy coping mechanisms.
   - **Improving Mental Well-Being:** Getting assistance allows individuals to navigate internal processes more effectively.

Resolution comes from finding solutions that work for you. These strategies promote a sense of achievement and being in control.

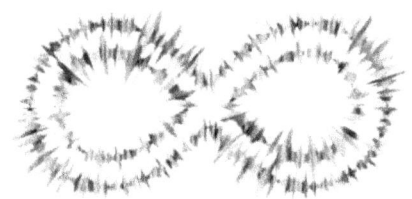

Expressing Sadness

Sadness is a natural process that everyone experiences at different points in their lives. In 1872, Charles Darwin proposed that emotions, including sadness, have evolutionary significance and play a vital role in human survival.

When we hold in our feelings of sorrow instead of expressing them, it can weigh heavily on our minds. This internal repression can lead to feelings of alienation and confusion, making it challenging to express ourselves honestly, even when we are alone.

When we are feeling sad, we may be more prone to engaging in critical thoughts and beliefs. For instance, we might doubt our abilities to perform well at work, constantly judge ourselves harshly for past mistakes, or believe we are not worthy of love and acceptance, leading to strained relationships. This can create barriers to effective communication by eroding our self-esteem and confidence.

Sadness can cloud our perspective, leading us to misinterpret information or jump to conclusions. We may find it difficult to articulate our needs.

Suppressing emotions can prevent us from engaging in open and honest communication. As a result, we may struggle to understand and address our innermost desires, which may lead to further distress.

When we are sad, we may avoid others, causing us to feel disconnected. This social withdrawal can limit our opportunities for external feedback and support. For example, we might stop reaching out to friends and family.

The lack of social interaction can intensify feelings of loneliness. It's important to note that these changes in our social behavior can also be a sign of depression, a heavy mental health concern that often co-occurs with prolonged sadness.

Signs to look out for:
- **Persistent Sadness:** If you've been feeling sad for an extended period, such as more than two weeks without any improvement, despite trying different strategies to feel better

- **Changes in Behavior:** Withdrawing from activities you once enjoyed, difficulty concentrating, alterations in appetite or sleep patterns, and excessive use of substances like alcohol and drugs as a way to cope with your feelings
- **Physical Symptoms:** Manifestations of headaches, stomach aches, fatigue, or other unexplained concerns

Causes of sadness:
- **Loss:** The death of a loved one, the end of a friendship, or moving away from home
- **Disappointment:** Not achieving a goal, failing a test, or feeling rejected
- **Loneliness:** Feeling alienated or disconnected from others
- **Stress:** Academic pressures, family issues, or personal problems

Tips:
1. **Talk About It:** Express your feelings to help lighten your mood.
2. **Engage in Activities:** Participate in hobbies, sports, or creative activities to distract and lift your spirit.
3. **Exercise:** Even a ten-minute walk can make a difference.
4. **Practice Mindfulness:** Meditation or deep breathing can help calm the mind.
5. **Establish a Routine:** A routine gives you a sense of control over your life. Include activities you enjoy that promote well-being, such as reading, hobbies, or spending time with family. Complete simple tasks like making your bed or preparing a healthy meal to create a sense of accomplishment.
6. **Connect with Nature:** Studies have shown that being outdoors can reduce feelings of sadness and improve mental health. Go for a walk in the park, hike a trail, or sit outside to enjoy the fresh air.
7. **Limit Screen Time:** While technology can offer some distractions, excessive screen time can also worsen feelings of sadness. Set boundaries for the amount of time spent on screens each day. Instead, use that time to engage in activities that promote your well-being, such as finishing tasks.
8. **Seek Professional Help:** If sadness persists or worsens, talking to a mental health professional can provide support and coping strategies. Asking for help is a sign of strength. When to seek help:
    - **Impact on Daily Life:** If your feelings of sadness are starting to affect your ability to function in your daily life, such as at school, with loved ones, or in other areas
    - **Thoughts of Self-Harm:** If you ever have thoughts of self-harm or suicide
    - **Difficulty Coping:** If you find it challenging to endure your emotions despite trying different coping strategies

Expressing Sadness

Sadness is a natural response to various situations and can help us process our feelings. It's okay to feel sad sometimes. Take care of your needs to reduce its impact.

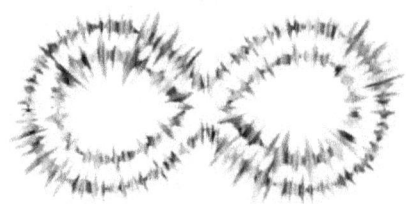

The Science of Tears:
More Than Just Emotion

Tears are often seen as a physical expression of sadness or grief. However, shedding tears serves various bodily functions beyond indicating our emotional state. Did you know that tears can also come from yawning, chopping onions, or feeling joyful? In the 1980s, a neuroscientist and researcher named Dr. William H. Frey II shed light on the composition of tears.

Tears are mainly produced by the lacrimal glands positioned above each eye. These glands continuously release a mixture of water, oils, mucus, and antibodies that collectively form tears.

While emotional tears are triggered by strong feelings, there are two other types of tears:
1. Basal tears
2. Reflex tears

Basal tears are continually produced to keep the eyes moist. They are also vital for delivering essential nutrients and oxygen to the cornea. This constant supply is crucial for maintaining clear vision and protecting our eyes from irritants like dust or smoke.

Reflex tears respond to external stimuli like chopping onions or when something gets in your eye. They help flush out irritants and foreign particles to keep the eyes clean and healthy.

In addition, tears contain stress hormones and toxins that the body needs to expel. Our bodies deliver cortisol when we experience stress from physical pain, frustration, or even when cutting onions. Crying can help remove them from the body while reducing feelings of distress.

Tears have antimicrobial properties. They can help fight off bacteria and keep our eyes clean. The lysozyme enzyme found in tears is a powerful weapon that can kill harmful bacteria. It minimizes the risk of eye infections and maintains ocular hygiene.

Sometimes, the pressure to achieve perfection can be overwhelming, leading to tears of frustration or disappointment. It's okay not to be perfect. Growth often comes from overcoming challenges and learning from mistakes.

Tears are remarkable fluids that reflect the complexity and beauty of the human body. Understanding their diverse functions encourages us to gain a deeper appreciation for these droplets. The next time you shed a tear, recall that it's your body's way of keeping you healthy and balanced.

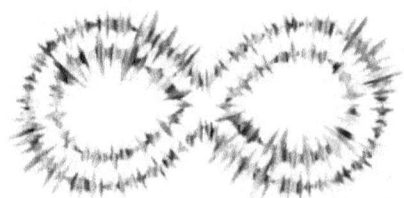

The Myth of Perfection

Perfection is a concept that many people strive for in several aspects of their lives. Whether it's wanting to achieve the perfect score on a test, the immaculate look, or the impeccable performance in an activity, the idea of being flawless can be alluring.

This unrealistic standard is impossible to achieve. The pursuit of perfection can have profound effects on our self-esteem, motivation, and overall well-being.

This concept has deep roots in human history. Numerous cultures and belief systems have shaped it over time. The idea of perfection can be tracked back to ancient societies such as the Greeks, Egyptians, and Chinese. It is often associated with gods, rulers, or natural phenomena.

One of the main reasons why perfection is unattainable is that it is a subjective and ever-changing concept. What may be considered perfect in one situation or by one person may not be seen as ideal by another. This variability means there is no universal standard for perfection, making it impossible to reach.

Comparison to a constantly shifting ideal can create a cycle of frustration and disappointment. For example, individuals may strive to be perfect at everything they do, only to feel deflated when they fall short of this unobtainable objective.

When individuals strive for perfection, they set themselves up for failure. Instead of celebrating their progress, they may focus solely on their perceived shortcomings. This negative self-talk can erode confidence.

Constantly striving to meet unrealistic standards can put immense pressure on individuals, leading to burnout and mental health issues. This burden can hinder reflection and communication because individuals may be too focused on their flaws to see their strengths.

When individuals are fixated on being flawless, it can lead to analysis paralysis. I like to call this over-analysis paralysis. They may evade taking risks or attempting new things out of fear of not meeting their impossibly high standards. It can stifle creativity, growth, and learning opportunities by impeding healthy expression and self-discovery.

Overly focusing on achieving perfection can spill over into how we talk to ourselves, creating a cycle of negativity and self-blame. It can also cause us to become hypercritical of those around us. This can lead to uneasy relationships and difficulty in forming genuine connections.

Utilize These Statements:
- Imperfection is a natural part of being human.
- Strive for progress rather than perfection.
- For every strength, there is an equally attached weakness.

Let go of unattainable standards by embracing flaws as learning experiences. Understanding this concept can be freeing. It's okay to be a work in progress. Actual growth comes from acceptance, resilience, and a willingness to learn from successes and setbacks.

This acceptance of imperfection allows for personal growth and self-love. It also creates a more inclusive and understanding community where everyone can feel valued for who they are. This sense of inclusivity and understanding can make individuals feel more connected and valued within their communities.

Just like how no two snowflakes are alike, each person is unique with their strengths and weaknesses. Nobody is perfect, and that is perfectly okay.

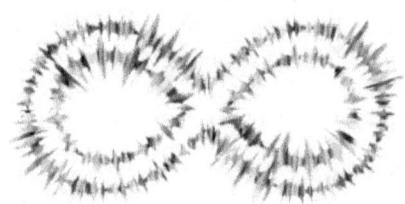

Reaching Acceptance

Acceptance is a powerful and transformative concept that implements a momentous transition in how we communicate with ourselves. When we reach a state of acceptance, we can better understand and acknowledge our thoughts, feelings, and experiences.

The idea of acceptance dates back to ancient times when communities were formed based on shared beliefs, traditions, and values. The importance of acceptance as a universal principle began to gain recognition in the 20th century.

One of the pioneers in promoting acceptance was Mahatma Gandhi, a leader known for advocating nonviolent resistance and social justice. Gandhi believed that acceptance of others, regardless of their background or beliefs, was essential for building a harmonious society.

We develop a more intimate understanding of ourselves when we accept who we are, including our strengths, weaknesses, and emotions. This allows us to engage in more honest and authentic internal conversations.

Research has shown that accepting all of our emotions creates space for genuine and open communication with ourselves. Instead of suppressing or denying our feelings, acceptance allows us to acknowledge them, process them, and find healthy ways to respond to them.

When we release the need to change facets of ourselves that are beyond our control, we liberate ourselves from self-sabotaging inner conflict. Practicing radical acceptance enables us to approach the reality of never-ending problems with a mindset focused on understanding and growth rather than frustration or avoidance.

The Reality of Facing Problems

We encounter multiple challenges and obstacles throughout life that test our perseverance and problem-solving skills. Feeling stressed or discouraged when faced with problems is normal, but avoiding or ignoring them will only lead to further complications.

Problems do not simply disappear on their own. For instance, if you have a leak in your roof, ignoring it may cause more damage to your home. Avoiding issues or shifting blame onto others only perpetuates a cycle of unresolved concerns.

Endless cycles of problems can be daunting, whether they are substantial global issues or personal challenges we face daily. It can sometimes feel overwhelming to even think about these problems, let alone take action to address them.

When faced with seemingly unsolvable problems, individuals may start projecting their biases and preconceptions onto the situation. This projection leads to a misinterpretation of common sense.

Evidence-based reasoning helps us make decisions based on factual evidence rather than personal beliefs. It helps individuals prevent misunderstandings so that they can arrive at well-informed conclusions.

Every complication presents a learning opportunity. When we actively engage in solving a problem, we develop critical thinking skills, resilience, and creativity. Promptly addressing dilemmas allows us to apply solutions.

Focusing on solutions empowers us to take control of our circumstances. Instead of feeling overwhelmed or helpless, we can approach problems with a positive mindset.

Shifting our perspective away from dwelling on the issue helps us regain confidence in overcoming obstacles. Ask yourself, "If I'm not going to do anything about resolving this problem in my life, then what's the point in focusing on it?"

While problems may be an inevitable part of life, how we approach them can make a significant difference. The real value lies not in the presence of problems but in our willingness to address them constructively.

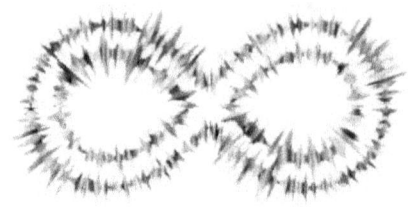

Common Sense:
A Worldwide Perspective

Common sense is the practical knowledge and reasoning that helps us navigate daily situations and make sound decisions. It involves using logic, experience, and intuition to solve problems so we can comprehend the world around us. This concept varies across diverse cultures and societies.

Let's explore the phrase "common sense is not so common." Our individual experiences, beliefs, and biases often shape common sense. This means that what may seem like common sense to one person may not be viewed the same way by another, especially when cultural conditioning and personal perspectives come into play.

The origins of common sense can be traced back to ancient societies such as Greece and Rome. In these civilizations, philosophers like Aristotle and Cicero spoke about a type of "common sense." It referred to a shared understanding of moral and ethical principles. This early concept of common sense was seen as an innate ability all humans possessed.

One of the fascinating aspects of common sense is its lack of universality. Each culture around the world has its unique set of norms, values, and ways of understanding the world.

What may be considered common sense in one culture may be entirely foreign or even regarded as nonsensical in another. For instance, the way we greet each other, communicate, or solve problems can vary significantly from one culture to another.

This diversity shows that common sense is not a fixed concept. Instead, it's a fluid and adaptable one. This understanding can inspire us to appreciate the cultural tapestry fabricating our world.

The environment in which we grow up, the values passed down by our families, and the societal norms we are exposed to all influence how we perceive common sense daily. Our personal biases can cloud our judgment and affect our ability to apply common sense effectively.

Common Sense: A Worldwide Perspective

When we look at the world through a "rose-colored lens," we tend to view things in a way that makes us feel better about ourselves or confirms our beliefs. This distortion of reality can prevent us from seeing situations clearly and objectively, leading to flawed decision-making and a lack of common sense.

Misunderstanding common sense may cause us to attribute our thoughts, feelings, or motives to others. This misinterpretation can lead to conflicts and inappropriate venting of frustrations. Recognizing our roles in shaping common sense can empower us to embrace unique perspectives.

Consider the diversity of experiences that shape our understanding of common sense to cultivate a more inclusive and empathetic mindset. This approach promotes a more harmonious and respectful global community.

Common sense is not a one-size-fits-all concept. Through mutual understanding and respect, we can deeply appreciate the richness and complexity that unites us as diverse global community members.

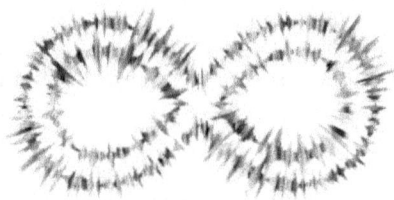

Venting Versus Self-Expression

When dealing with our emotions, it's imperative to understand the difference between venting and healthy self-expression. Both ways help release feelings but have distinct characteristics and outcomes.

Venting is when we release our emotions without considering how they may impact others or ourselves. It often involves expressing our feelings in a raw and unfiltered manner. Sometimes, it occurs impulsively or aggressively. Venting can take various forms, such as ranting to a friend, writing a heated post on social media, or even yelling and slamming doors.

Venting that lasts less than one minute is within the standard range for this habit. However, if venting persists for one to five minutes, it may indicate a deeper level of distress and raise concerns about emotional well-being. Venting that extends beyond five minutes is a sign that professional intervention from a mental health practitioner may be necessary to address underlying issues and provide support.

When someone has a habit of venting about their day, it can sometimes lead to them becoming a conversational narcissist. This transformation occurs when the person consistently lacks genuine interest in engaging others' thoughts or feelings during conversation. Over time, this behavior creates a one-sided conversational dynamic where the person's need to talk about themselves constantly overshadows any meaningful two-way communication.

While venting may provide temporary relief, knowing its potential consequences is worthwhile. Venting without boundaries can escalate conflicts, strain relationships, and reinforce negative emotions. It may not address the root cause of our feelings and can lead to a cycle of frustration.

The drawbacks of venting for prolonged periods:

- **Rumination:** Venting for too long about a negative experience can lead to constantly replaying the situation in our minds. This can deepen negative emotions and prevent us from moving forward.

- **Validation Seeking:** Spending excessive time venting can sometimes turn into seeking validation rather than genuinely working through our feelings. This propensity can form a cycle of dependency on others for emotional support.
- **Misinterpretation:** If not done constructively, others can misinterpret venting. It may come across as complaining or overly pessimistic, impacting how others perceive us.
- **Energy Drain:** Constant venting without taking action toward solutions can drain our energy. It may leave us feeling stuck in a cycle of negativity without making any progress towards feeling better.

Healthy self-expression involves expressing our emotions productively. It is about finding ways to communicate how we feel while considering the impact on ourselves and those around us. Healthy self-expression encourages self-awareness, empathy, and effective communication skills.

Journaling, talking to a trusted person, creating art, or practicing mindfulness are forms of healthy expression. They allow us to process our emotions, gain insights into our feelings, and find practical solutions to manage challenges. Rather than just releasing emotions, healthy self-expression promotes healing, growth, and emotional well-being, making it a valuable tool for our personal development.

Key differences:
- **Intention:** Venting is often impulsive and reactive. Healthy self-expression is intentional and mindful.
- **Outcome:** Venting may temporarily release emotions but can lead to negative consequences. Healthy self-expression fosters emotional growth and resilience.
- **Impact:** Venting may strain relationships and escalate conflicts. Healthy self-expression promotes understanding and connection.
- **Reflection:** Venting lacks reflection and self-awareness. Healthy self-expression encourages introspection and personal growth.

Tips for healthy self-expression:
1. **Reflect Before You React:** Take a moment to process your feelings before expressing them.
2. **Choose Your Methods:** Find creative outlets that resonate with you, such as writing, drawing, or exercising.
3. **Practice Empathy:** Consider how your words and actions may impact others before expressing yourself.
4. **Seek Support:** Establish a trusting relationship with a mental health provider to ensure that you receive reliable support and guidance. This will lead to outcomes that are in your best interest. Avoid unqualified individuals because they may not have the knowledge or skills to help you effectively.

When people vent without considering the impact of their words, it can lead to misunderstandings and criticism from others. Feeling and expressing your emotions is okay, but doing so constructively and mindfully can lead to positive outcomes. Like a volcano that needs to release pressure to prevent a catastrophic eruption, thoughtful expression can help avert negative consequences.

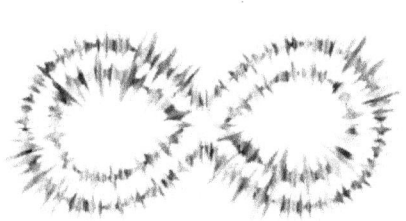

Recognizing Triggers

Triggers are events, circumstances, or thoughts that can cause a person to have a strong emotional reaction. Trauma responses can vary, including anger, sadness, anxiety, and fear. Trauma responses are related to the work of Hans Selye, a Hungarian-Canadian endocrinologist. In the 1930s, Selye began researching how the body reacts to stress. He introduced the General Adaptation Syndrome (GAS), a model that describes how the body responds to stress in three stages.

Trauma occurs during a distressing event that overwhelms a person's ability to cope. This overwhelming experience can lead to intense feelings of fear, helplessness, or horror.

Main Types of Trauma:
1. **Acute Trauma:** This type of trauma results from a single event. For example, experiencing a car accident or witnessing an act of violence. People may experience symptoms like shock, confusion, and difficulty sleeping immediately following the event.
2. **Chronic Trauma:** This occurs when a person faces repeated and prolonged exposure to distressing events, such as ongoing abuse, neglect, or living in a war zone. The effects of chronic trauma can be more profound and long-lasting, impacting a person's overall mental health and interpersonal relationships.

The Trauma Cycle:
- **Alarm Phase:** In this initial stage, the body reacts to the trauma as if it is in danger. This response is often referred to as the survival response. Hormones like cortisol and adrenaline are released, preparing the body to confront or escape the threat. This can lead to symptoms such as elevated heart rate, rapid breathing, and heightened senses.

- **Resistance Phase:** After the initial shock, individuals may attempt to cope with the trauma. They might use various strategies to distract themselves, such as talking to friends or engaging in enjoyable activities. However, if the trauma is too overwhelming, individuals can become stuck in this stage, leading to feelings of anxiety, depression, or anger.
- **Exhaustion Phase:** If stress continues for too long without relief, individuals can enter the exhaustion phase. Feelings of hopelessness, fatigue, and withdrawal characterize this stage. People may find it hard to function in daily life while experiencing distress.

Common Responses:
1. **Fight response** is one way our body prepares to deal with danger. When we feel threatened, our brain sends signals to prepare us for action. This response can make us feel energized and ready to confront the threat. For example, if a student feels bullied at school, they might become angry and prepared to stand up for themselves.
2. **Flight response** is another reaction during the alarm phase. Instead of fighting, some people might feel the urge to escape a situation. This response is driven by the desire to avoid danger. Someone who sees a big dog running toward them might run away to feel safe. This instinct is natural, and it helps keep us safe from harm. However, if someone constantly feels the need to run away from challenges, it might impact their personal growth.
3. **Freeze response** occurs when individuals experience overwhelming fear. This reaction can make a person feel paralyzed or unable to move. It's as if their body is in shock. Think of a deer caught in the headlights of a vehicle. It can lead to feelings of helplessness.
4. **Fawn response** is fulfilled by a desire to please others to avoid conflict. People who experience this response might go out of their way to make others feel comfortable, often at the expense of their own needs. For example, someone may agree with a group to fit in, even if it means ignoring their feelings. This can make it challenging to maintain self-respect and personal boundaries.
5. **Anger responses** may emerge as frustration or rage. For example, a person who feels neglected might lash out at friends or family. It can be a signal that something needs to be addressed. Finding healthy outlets for anger, such as engaging in physical activity, can be beneficial.
6. **Dissociation response** happens when a person feels detached from reality or their surroundings. It might feel like they are watching themselves from the outside. For instance, a student may daydream or zone out during a stressful class. Frequent episodes may indicate a need for support or intervention.

7. **Hyperarousal response** is a state of heightened alertness. Someone may feel anxious, irritable, or easily startled. They might find it hard to concentrate or feel jumpy at loud noises. This response keeps individuals on high alert for potential threats but can lead to fatigue if it occurs too often.

Trauma effects can manifest in different ways. They can also vary in intensity and duration. Here are some common trauma symptoms:

- **Emotional:** Individuals may experience a range of emotions, including sadness, anger, guilt, or confusion. These feelings can be overwhelming and may change from day to day or even hour to hour.
- **Cognitive:** Trauma can affect a person's thinking. They might have difficulty concentrating, remembering details, or making decisions. In some cases, they may re-experience the event through flashbacks or intrusive thoughts.
- **Physical:** Individuals may suffer from headaches, stomach aches, or chronic pain. Some people may turn to coping mechanisms, such as substance abuse, to manage their physical and emotional pain.
- **Behavioral:** Changes in behavior are common after trauma. Individuals may become withdrawn or avoid anything that reminds them of the traumatic event. Others might become more aggressive or engage in risky behaviors.

Triggers are unique to each person. What may trigger one individual may not have the same effect on another. Intentional questions help us uncover the underlying reasons behind our emotional reactions. Instead of reacting to a trigger, we can pause and ask ourselves questions that prompt introspection.

Examples:
- What thoughts were going through my mind when I experienced this trigger?
- How did my body physically react to the trigger?
- Have I experienced a similar trigger in the past? How did I respond then?
- What is the worst-case scenario that I am imagining in this situation?
- Are there any underlying beliefs influencing my reaction to this trigger?

Asking these types of questions helps us gain insight into our thought processes, patterns of behavior, and other contributions to our emotional responses. For example, let's say someone feels anxious whenever they have to speak in front of a group. Asking intentional questions can help them discover that their fear stems from a belief that they are not good enough or a past negative experience in a similar situation.

Identifying these underlying factors allows individuals to work towards challenging and reframing their beliefs. Devoting a few moments each day to ask ourselves intentional questions can help us become more accustomed to our emotions and reactions.

Recovering from trauma is a personal journey, and it often requires support from others. Here are some ways individuals can find healing:
- **Therapy**: Professional help from a psychologist or counselor can be invaluable. Therapists can provide coping strategies, help individuals process their emotions, and guide them through their recovery journey.
- **Support Groups**: Connecting with others who have experienced similar traumas can provide comfort and understanding. Support groups create a safe space for individuals to share their feelings and experiences.
- **Self-Care**: Taking care of one's physical and emotional health is crucial. This can include regular exercise, healthy eating, and practicing relaxation techniques like meditation or deep breathing.
- **Building a Support System**: Friends and family can play a vital role in recovery. Having a strong support system can help individuals feel less isolated and more understood.

Taking a step back in moments of heightened emotions can help us pause and respond thoughtfully. Over time, this method can lead to improved emotional regulation and more effective communication with ourselves and others.

Recovery from trauma is possible. Learning to identify triggers empowers us with indispensable knowledge. Recognizing them in the communication process can provide valuable clues about underlying insecurities that may be at play. With the right tools and support, individuals can move forward and regain control of their lives.

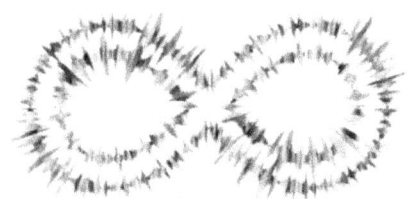

Signs of Insecurity

Insecurity is a prevalent feeling that many people experience at some point in their lives. It can enforce how a person behaves, interacts with others, and views themselves. British psychologist John Bowlby contributed to the development of attachment theory in 1969.

Attachment theory suggests that a child's early relationships with caregivers profoundly impact their emotional development and future relationships. Bowlby suggested that a secure attachment to caregivers during infancy lays the foundation for healthy emotional development. In contrast, insecure attachments can lead to feelings of insecurity and anxiety later in life.

Attachment Styles:
1. **Secure attachment** is considered the healthiest attachment style. Children with a secure attachment feel safe and supported by their caregivers. They trust their needs will be resolved and are comfortable exploring their environment. When their caregiver leaves the room, they may feel some distress, but they are easily comforted when the caregiver returns.

    Secure attachment styles tend to have stable relationships as adults. They communicate well with partners, express their needs, and handle conflicts effectively. They are also more likely to support their loved ones and seek help when needed.
2. **Anxiously attached** individuals often worry about their relationships. As children, they might have experienced inconsistent caregiving, where their needs were sometimes met and sometimes ignored. This inconsistency can lead to anxiety. When separated from their caregivers, these children may become very upset and have difficulty calming down once the caregiver returns.

    Anxious attachment styles often crave closeness and reassurance from their partners. They may fear abandonment and often over-analyze their relationships. This can lead to clinginess or excessive need for validation, which can strain relationships.

3. **Avoidant attachment** develops when caregivers are emotionally unavailable or unresponsive. Children with this attachment style learn to rely on themselves rather than their caregivers. They often suppress their feelings and may appear indifferent when separated from their caregiver. These children may not seek comfort when upset and instead focus on exploring their surroundings.

    Avoidant attachment styles value independence and may struggle with intimacy. They often avoid getting too close to others and may struggle to express their emotions. This can lead to challenges in romantic relationships because they may appear distant or emotionally unavailable.

4. **Disorganized attachment** is a combination of anxious and avoidant styles. It often occurs in situations where caregivers are a source of both comfort and fear, such as in cases of abuse or neglect. Children with this attachment style may show conflicting behaviors. They might approach their caregiver for comfort but then pull away in fear. This inconsistency can be very confusing for the child.

    Disorganized attachment styles may struggle with their relationships as adults. They may have difficulty trusting others and often experience high levels of anxiety. Unpredictable behaviors and emotional swings can mark their relationships.

Reflecting on our attachment styles can help us identify patterns in our relationships. For example, if someone consistently finds themselves in unstable relationships, they might explore their attachment style and consider how it affects their choices.

Insecurity indicates a lack of confidence or assurance in oneself. When someone is insecure, they may doubt their abilities, feel anxious about how others perceive them, or constantly seek validation from others. Insecurity can manifest in various ways.

Signs of Insecurity:
- **Constant Need for Reassurance:** Insecure Individuals persistently validate their worth through others. They may frequently ask for approval or confirmation of their actions and decisions.
- **Comparing Themselves to Others:** Insecure individuals focus on perceived shortcomings or flaws. This perpetual comparison can lead to feelings of inadequacy and self-doubt.
- **Avoiding Challenges:** Insecure people may avoid taking on new challenges or risks out of fear of failure. They may doubt their abilities to succeed and prefer to stay within their comfort zones.
- **Overly Apologetic:** Insecure individuals may apologize excessively, even for minor things that are not their fault. This behavior stems from a fear of upsetting others or being perceived negatively.

- **Difficulty Accepting Compliments:** When someone is insecure, they may downplay their achievements or feel unworthy of praise.
- **Perfectionism:** Insecurity can lead to perfectionist tendencies, where individuals strive for unattainable standards to prove their worth. This persistent pursuit of perfection can be exhausting and damaging to self-esteem.
- **Negative Self-Talk:** Insecure individuals often use negative self-talk by rebuking themselves. This internal dialogue can contribute to feelings of worthlessness.
- **Seeking External Validation:** Insecure individuals may rely heavily on external validation, such as social media likes, compliments, or material possessions.
- **Avoiding Eye Contact:** Insecure people may avoid initiating eye contact during conversations or interactions. This avoidance can stem from shame, inadequacy, or fear of judgment.
- **Difficulty Making Decisions:** Insecurity can lead to indecisiveness. Individuals may second-guess themselves or rely on others to make decisions for them out of fear of making the wrong choice.

Insecurities can cause individuals to project thoughts and feelings onto others. This projection serves as a defense mechanism for attributes they feel they lack. Projecting their fears onto others enables individuals to alleviate their feelings of inadequacy temporarily.

Everyone experiences moments of insecurity. Recognizing the signs of insecurity in yourself and others is prominent for building confidence. Working towards secure attachment creates loving and supportive relationships that enrich our lives.

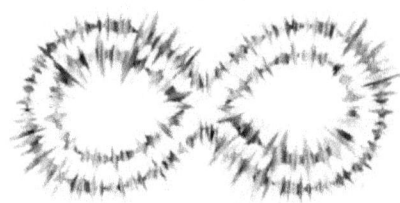

Realizing Projection

Projection occurs when individuals attribute their feelings, thoughts, or impulses to another person. It happens when we see in others what we don't want to see in ourselves. Sigmund Freud proposed the idea of projection as a defense mechanism in his work on psychoanalytic theory during the 19th and 20th centuries. According to Freud, projection is a way for individuals to protect themselves from acknowledging their undesirable traits.

Signs of Projecting Onto Others:
- **Blaming Others Unfairly:** One of the primary signs of projection is unjustly blaming others for things that are our responsibility. For example, if someone consistently accuses others of being dishonest, they may struggle with telling the truth.
- **Overreacting to Criticism:** When we project, we might lash out at others for feedback that hits too close to home. It can be much easier to be defensive than to face our flaws.
- **Obsessive Judgment:** Criticizing others can be a way of protecting our insecurities. Pointing out flaws in others enables us to avoid looking at our shortcomings.
- **Feeling Irrationally Threatened:** If we feel unreasonably threatened or intimidated by someone, it could be a sign that we are projecting our fears onto them. This often stems from our unresolved concerns.

Signs of Being Projected Onto:
- **Feeling Misunderstood:** When someone projects onto us, we might feel like they don't see us for who we are. They are more focused on their issues rather than understanding us.
- **Confusion:** Being on the receiving end of projection can be confusing. We might find ourselves unsure of why someone is reacting to us in a certain way, especially if their behavior seems disproportionate to the situation.

- **Defensiveness:** If someone projects their issues onto us, we may become defensive or reactive. We can take a step back and consider whether their accusations pertain to us or if they are projecting their issues.
- **Feeling Drained:** Interacting with someone projecting onto us can be exhausting. Their projections can weigh heavily on us and affect our self-esteem.

Dealing With Projection:
- When you catch yourself projecting onto others, take a moment to reflect on where it's coming from. Self-awareness is fundamental to fracturing the cycle of projection.
- When someone is projecting onto you, approach the situation with empathy and understanding. Their projections are more about them than they are about you. Set boundaries and communicate openly to help mitigate the impact of their projections on your well-being.

Projecting negative emotions can hinder effective communication and escalate conflicts, resulting in misunderstandings and hurt feelings. Be mindful of reactions when engaging with others.

Understanding the signs of projection helps us to navigate various situations, including online and offline. This knowledge empowers us to develop a deeper understanding of ourselves and others.

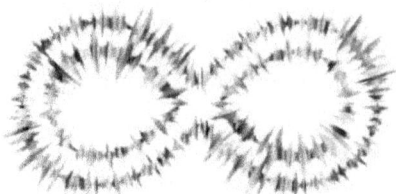

Aggressive Communication

Aggressive communication is a way of expressing oneself that involves being forceful, pushy, or hostile. It can ignite tension and conflict in relationships. John Doe was a pioneering psychologist in the early 20th century who delved into the complexities of human behavior and communication patterns. In his research, he observed that some individuals tended to express themselves in ways that were perceived as confrontational, intimidating, or disrespectful.

Signs of Aggressive Communication:
- **Verbal aggression** involves harsh words, yelling, insults, or threats to intimidate or control others. It can lead to fear or insecurity in the person on the receiving end.
- **Passive-aggressive behavior** is characterized by indirect expressions of hostility or negativity. It can involve sarcasm, silent treatment, or backhanded compliments. While the aggression is not explicitly stated, it is still present in the form of subtle digs and manipulation.
- **Hostile body language** includes gestures like pointing fingers, crossed arms, glaring eyes, or invading personal space. These nonverbal cues can escalate conflict.
- **Defensive communication** involves reacting to perceived threats with hostility. Instead of listening and understanding, defensive communicators may deflect blame, make excuses, or attack the other person. It can hinder productive dialogue and problem-solving.
- **Blaming and accusations** occur without taking responsibility for their actions. They may use phrases like "You always..." or "You never..." to shift blame and avoid accountability.

Aggressive communication can erode trust, create a hostile environment, and damage self-esteem. It often leads to misunderstandings and conflicts.

Tips:
1. **Stay Calm:** When faced with aggressive communication, it is necessary to remain calm and composed. Responding in a similarly aggressive manner can escalate the situation further.
2. **Set Boundaries:** Establishing clear boundaries and communicating them assertively can help deter aggressive behavior from others.
3. **Use "I" Statements:** Frame your responses using "I" statements. They allow the expression of thoughts and feelings without sounding accusatory. Avoid using "you" as much as possible unless it's necessary and does not emphasize blame.
4. **Seek Support:** When in doubt, always seek assistance from a qualified professional you can rely on.

Understanding the different forms of aggression is a transformative journey that empowers us to advocate for ourselves. Promote open and respectful communication to create a more harmonious environment for everyone involved.

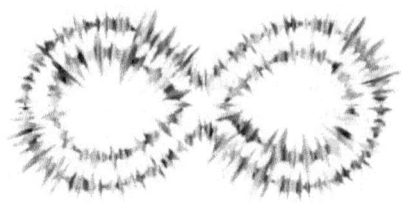

Setting Limits

Healthy boundaries are like an invisible line that separates your thoughts, feelings, and needs from those of others. They define what is acceptable and unacceptable in your interactions. In Greek philosophy, thinkers like Aristotle and Plato discussed the idea of defining personal space. Boundaries help establish one's identity and communicate one's values.

Limits help create a balance between giving and receiving in relationships. They protect you from being taken advantage of or mistreated by others. Knowing when to set boundaries is vital for preventing burnout and resentment. Before establishing boundaries, make sure you fully understand what occurs in a situation through intentional questions.

Once you have a complete understanding of the situation and the underlying intentions, you may need boundaries. They can be created when you feel uncomfortable, disrespected, or overwhelmed. Listen to your feelings and intuition because they can guide you in recognizing when your boundaries are being crossed.

Signs of Needing Boundaries:
- Feeling stressed or anxious in certain situations
- Constantly saying yes to things you don't want to do
- Not having time for yourself due to excessive commitments
- Feeling drained or depleted after interacting with particular individuals

Tips:
1. **Identify Your Limits:** Take the time to reflect on your needs, values, and comfort levels. What are you willing to accept? What crosses the line for you?
2. **Communicate Clearly:** Express yourself in a straightforward and assertive manner. Use "I" statements to convey your needs without blaming or accusing others. For example, "I feel uncomfortable when spoken to in that tone."

3. **Be Firm and Consistent:** Once you've established your boundaries, stick to them consistently. Do not allow others to violate your limits. Be prepared to follow through with consequences if necessary.
4. **Practice Self-Care:** Setting boundaries also means caring for yourself physically, emotionally, and mentally. Prioritize self-care activities that rejuvenate your energy to restore balance in your life.
5. **Seek Support:** Consult someone knowledgeable and experienced in this subject matter to provide accurate information and guidance customized to your needs.

Boundaries are not selfish. They are a sign of self-respect and self-love. Knowing your limits is indispensable and leads to a more fulfilling life.

Personal Boundaries

Personal boundaries are the guidelines we set for ourselves regarding our thoughts, feelings, and behaviors. They involve recognizing our limits, understanding our needs, and respecting ourselves enough to uphold those parameters.

In ancient Greece, the philosopher Socrates emphasized the importance of self-awareness and self-control. He believed that individuals should know their limits and respect the boundaries of others.

We may feel overwhelmed, stressed, or taken advantage of when we lack boundaries. Understanding and implementing boundaries can increase self-esteem, better decision-making, and a more balanced life.

Types:
- **Physical boundaries** involve how we treat our bodies.
- **Sexual boundaries** include limits that we set regarding our own body and sexual activity.
- **Mental boundaries** consist of the thoughts we permit in our mind.
- **Emotional boundaries** define how we allow circumstances to affect our feelings.
- **Spiritual boundaries** help us establish what we believe is acceptable.
- **Personal value boundaries** represent our actions towards things that are important to us.
- **Time boundaries** are set regarding how we spend our time.
- **Legal boundaries** determine how we allow ourselves to behave according to laws and regulations set by the government.
- **Material boundaries** relate to how you treat your belongings and resources.
- **Digital boundaries** refer to the limits we set regarding how we engage with technology.

Benefits of Boundaries:
- **Self-Preservation:** Boundaries protect our well-being. They help us identify what is acceptable and what is not.
- **Self-Respect:** When we set boundaries, we value our needs and feelings. This self-respect encourages others to treat us with the same regard.
- **Self-Love:** Establishing boundaries allows us to fulfill our needs.
- **Focus:** We can prioritize our time and energy. This means we can dedicate ourselves to what truly matters to us, whether it's school, hobbies, or self-care.

Tips:
1. **Know Yourself:** Reflect on what makes you feel comfortable and what doesn't. Consider the following questions.
   - What situations make me feel stressed or anxious?
   - Are there certain people who drain my energy?
   - What do I enjoy doing, and how can I make time for those activities?
2. **Communicate Clearly:** Use "I" statements to express your feelings and needs. For example:
   - "I feel overwhelmed when I take on too many responsibilities. I need to say no to some requests."
   - "I need some alone time to recharge. Can we plan to hang out later?"
3. **Start Small:** If setting boundaries feels daunting, start with small changes. You can practice saying no to minor requests or taking breaks when overwhelmed. Gradually, you can build up to more significant boundaries. This approach will help you gain confidence in maintaining your limits.
4. **Be Consistent:** Once you've established a boundary, stick to it. If you allow your limits to be pushed, it can cause internal conflict. Being consistent reinforces the importance of your boundaries.
5. **Practice Self-Care:** Make self-care a priority. Employ activities that bring you joy and relaxation, such as reading or exercising.
6. **Be Prepared for Pushback:** Sometimes, we may not respond positively to our boundaries. We might feel disappointed or conflicted. Be prepared for this possibility and stand firm in your decisions. Your boundaries are for your well-being. It's okay to prioritize your needs.
7. **Reflect and Adjust:** As you practice setting boundaries, reflect on what works and what doesn't. Alter any boundaries that are not serving you well. Personal growth is an ongoing process, and your boundaries may evolve as you do.

Setting healthy boundaries is not selfish. It is a mandatory part of self-love. Start identifying your needs so you can establish your personal limits. As you implement these strategies, you will likely see improvements in your mental health, relationships, and overall happiness.

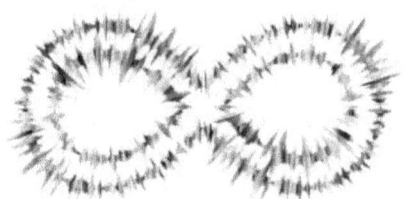

Rigid Boundaries

Rigid personal boundaries refer to the strict limits we impose on ourselves. Being inflexible prevents us from experiencing life fully. The concept of rigid boundaries in psychology can be applied to the pioneering work of renowned psychologist Karen Horney.

Through her extensive research and clinical work, Horney delved into the complex dynamics of human relationships and identified rigid boundaries as a critical factor in understanding behavior.

In 1937, Horney theorized that individuals with rigid boundaries tend to be defensive and inflexible in their approach to relationships, often keeping others at a distance emotionally. These individuals may struggle to form close connections with others and may exhibit a strong need for control and independence. Horney's work shed light on how these rigid boundaries can impact an individual's well-being and social interactions.

Imagine a wall so high and thick that nothing can get through. This wall represents rigid boundaries. While boundaries are necessary for protection, being too rigid can isolate us from others and limit our opportunities.

For instance, if someone decides never to share their feelings with anyone, they create a rigid emotional boundary. While this might protect them from vulnerability, it also prevents them from forming deep connections with friends and family. These restrictions can lead to loneliness and frustration.

Common Signs:
- **Difficulty Accepting Help:** Individuals may feel that needing assistance is a sign of weakness. They often believe they must handle everything independently, leading to increased stress.
- **Avoiding Vulnerability:** Someone may think sharing personal feelings and experiences makes them weak or exposes them to judgment. This avoidance can prevent deeper connections with friends and family because relationships often thrive on trust and openness.

- **Controlling Behavior:** Individuals might try to dictate how others should behave. This desire can stem from a fear of being hurt or disappointed. This behavior can create tension and conflict in relationships.
- **Difficulty Compromising:** Individuals may struggle to see other perspectives or find common ground. This can make it challenging to work collaboratively with others, whether in school, work, or personal relationships.
- **Emotional Shutdown:** People with rigid boundaries might suppress their feelings instead of expressing them. This can lead to loneliness and alienation because they may appear unapproachable or indifferent to others.
- **Fear of Intimacy:** Some people avoid close relationships because they are afraid of being hurt or betrayed. This can cause them to push others away, leading to a lack of meaningful connections.
- **Negative Self-Perception:** Individuals may feel unworthy of love and support. They believe they must always be strong and self-sufficient, which can create a cycle of unhappiness.

One reason people establish rigid boundaries is to protect themselves. Perhaps they have faced hurt or disappointment, leading them to believe that keeping others at a distance will shield them from further pain. While it's natural to want to protect ourselves, overly rigid boundaries can cause more harm than good.

For example, let's consider a student who decides not to join any clubs or activities at school because they fear rejection. This student might feel safe from disappointment, but they also miss out on chances to make friends and explore new interests.

When we refuse to let others in, we may miss the chance to build meaningful connections. Friends and family members might feel shut out or rejected, leading to misunderstandings and conflicts.

Think about a scenario where a teenager decides not to talk about their struggles. They might believe that discussing their challenges will make them look weak. However, this lack of communication can strain relationships with those who care about them. Friends may feel helpless, while the teenager may feel increasingly sad.

Having flexible boundaries allows for open communication. This means being able to share feelings and experiences while still protecting oneself.

Ask yourself questions like:
- What am I protecting myself from?
- Are these boundaries helping or hindering my relationships?
- How can I adjust my boundaries to allow for growth and connection?

When we identify the reasons behind our boundaries, we can begin to adjust them. Flexible boundaries are adaptable. They allow us to change how we interact with others based on the situation. For example, someone might feel comfortable sharing their thoughts with a close friend but may choose to keep specific topics private in a larger group.

Benefits of Flexible Boundaries:
- **Improved Relationships:** Being open to communication and sharing feelings fosters deeper connections.
- **Increased Self-Awareness:** Understanding our needs and limits helps us become more in tune with ourselves.
- **Better Emotional Health:** Allowing ourselves to express feelings can reduce stress and anxiety.
- **Opportunities for Growth:** Flexible boundaries enable us to try new experiences without the fear of being overwhelmed.

Tips:
1. **Define Your Priorities:** Take some time to consider what is most important to you. Are your academic goals your top priority? Do you want to make time for hobbies or social activities? Understanding what matters most will help you determine where to set boundaries.

    Once you have identified your priorities, write them down. Having a clear list can remind you of what you are working toward. For example, if your priority is to maintain good grades, you might set a limit to only allow screen time after you complete your homework.
2. **Create a Schedule:** A schedule provides structure to your day and helps you allocate time for different activities. When you have a set plan, it is easier to stick to your boundaries.

    List all your responsibilities, including schoolwork, chores, and personal activities. Afterward, allocate time slots for each task. Be sure to include breaks to recharge. For instance, you might schedule two hours for studying and a 30-minute break. Stick to this schedule as closely as possible, and treat these time blocks as non-negotiable.
3. **Use Positive Reinforcement:** Reward yourself for fulfilling your objectives. This can help motivate you to maintain discipline.

    For example, if you successfully study for your scheduled hours without distractions, treat yourself to a snack or an episode of a show. Choosing rewards that you genuinely enjoy encourages you to keep following your priorities.
4. **Identify Triggers:** For example, if you notice that social media distracts you when trying to study, consider setting a boundary of only checking social media during breaks. Alternatively, you can use apps that limit your access to certain sites during study times. Recognizing your triggers and taking proactive steps can help you maintain your needs more effectively.

5. **Stay Accountable:** Sharing your aspirations with someone you trust can help you stay committed. When someone knows about your needs, they can offer support and encouragement.

   Consider setting up regular check-ins with your accountability partner to discuss your progress. This will keep you responsible for your actions and allow you to celebrate your progress.

Rigid boundaries can limit our experiences in life. While protecting yourself is valuable, be open to growth and connection. This balance is critical to building fulfillment.

It may take time to adjust to new boundaries, but the effort will pay off in the long run. Discipline and determination empower you to achieve your needs.

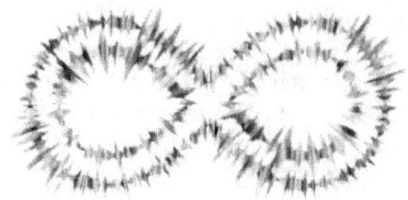

Diffuse Boundaries

Introduced by Erik Erikson in 1950, diffuse boundaries are the opposite of rigid boundaries. They occur when an individual has difficulty distinguishing between their own needs and the needs of others. This can lead to feeling overwhelmed, stressed, or even resentful.

For instance, a person with diffuse boundaries might constantly prioritize the needs of friends or family over their own, leading to exhaustion and frustration. They might also struggle to say "no" to requests, fearing they will disappoint others or face conflict.

Setting boundaries empowers us to sustain a healthy and balanced life. However, for many people, boundaries can sometimes feel unclear, especially when it comes to personal limits. The lines between what is acceptable and what is not become blurred.

Signs of Diffuse Boundaries:
- **Lack of Personal Space:** Someone may not have enough time or room to think and reflect.
- **Difficulty Saying No:** Individuals may take on more responsibilities or tasks than they can handle.
- **Feeling Drained or Resentful:** It can be challenging to prioritize their needs and well-being, leading to negative emotions.
- **Blurred Sense of Self:** Maintaining a clear sense of self can be challenging, leading to confusion about personal identity and values.
- **Difficulty Establishing Limits:** Individuals may struggle to maintain limits, leading to a lack of control over their time, energy, and resources.
- **Seeking Validation from Others:** This can result in a dependence on external sources for validating their self-esteem rather than cultivating confidence and self-worth.
- **Tolerance of Disrespectful Behavior:** When individuals do not assert their boundaries or consequences, they may inadvertently signal that such behavior is acceptable.

- **Difficulty Expressing Emotions:** Some people struggle to assert their emotions, leading to repressed feelings or explosive outbursts.
- **Internal Conflict**: When individuals do not enforce clear values, it can create internal chaos and self-doubt.

Benefits of Healthy Boundaries:
- **Self-Care:** When you prioritize your needs, you can better support others.
- **Healthy Relationships:** Clear boundaries allow you to communicate your needs and expectations, leading to more trust and respect.
- **Emotional Well-Being:** Establishing boundaries can reduce feelings of anxiety and stress. Knowing your limits allows you to make decisions that align with your values and priorities.
- **Personal Growth:** You create space for new opportunities that align with your goals.

Tips:
1. **Identify Your Needs and Values:** Spend some time reflecting on what is important to you. Ask yourself questions like:
   - What makes me feel happy and fulfilled?
   - What are my non-negotiables in life?
   - How do I want to be treated by others?
2. **Implement "No":** Start by saying "no" to small requests that don't align with your priorities. This will help you build confidence to decline larger requests in the future.
3. **Communicate Clearly and Assertively:** Use "I" statements to express your needs without blaming others. For example, instead of saying, "They always ask too much of me," you could say, "I need some time for myself and can't take on any more tasks right now." This approach helps you express your feelings while maintaining respect for others.
4. **Be Consistent:** If you do not set and enforce a boundary, how are others supposed to take it seriously? Stick to your boundaries even when they feel uncomfortable. Over time, it will become easier to respect your limits.
5. **Reflect and Adjust as Needed:** Regularly reflect on your boundaries. Are they still serving you well? Do you need to adjust any of them? Being flexible and willing to change your boundaries as your needs evolve is integral to self-care.
6. **Seek Support:** Talking about your challenges with qualified people can encourage you, help you gain perspective, and motivate you to stick to your boundaries.

It's okay to prioritize yourself. Change is possible, and it starts with you. Set boundaries that positively influence your well-being.

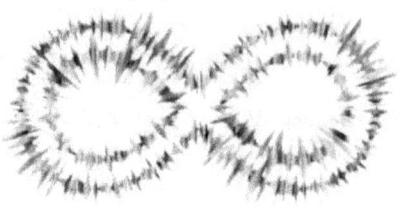

How to Say No

Knowing when and how to say no is pertinent when peer pressure and social expectations are prevalent. Saying no assertively means standing up for yourself, setting boundaries, and making decisions without feeling guilty.

In ancient Greece, personal agency and self-determination were highly valued. Philosophers like Socrates and Aristotle emphasized the importance of individual autonomy and the ability to make choices based on one's values and beliefs. Their teachings helped shape the concept of saying "no" as a form of self-expression.

There are many situations where saying no assertively is crucial. For example, if someone is pressuring you to engage in risky behavior that goes against your core values, saying no assertively can help you make choices that align with your true self.

Saying no is not just about rejecting requests. It is about respecting your own needs and limits.

Benefits:
- **Protecting Your Time:** We all have busy schedules filled with school, homework, extracurricular activities, and personal time. Saying no to unnecessary commitments frees up time for what truly matters to you.
- **Maintaining Mental Health:** Overcommitting can lead to stress and burnout. Learning to say no can help you manage your self-care and reduce anxiety. When you are not overloaded with commitments, you will likely feel less stressed and more in control of your life.
- **Building Self-Confidence:** When you assertively say no, you advocate for yourself. This can empower you in other areas of life, from academics to personal relationships.
- **Establishing Boundaries:** Saying no helps set clear boundaries. It communicates your limits, leading to healthier relationships where your needs are respected.

Tips:
1. **Be Direct:** Use clear and straightforward language to express your decision. Avoid giving mixed signals or lengthy explanations. A simple "No, I can't do that" is often sufficient. It shows that you are serious about your decision.
2. **Use "I" Statements:** Frame your response utilizing "I" statements. For example, using statements like "I feel uncomfortable with that," "I'm not going to," or "I feel overwhelmed with my current responsibilities."
3. **Stay Calm and Confident:** When saying no, maintain a calm and composed demeanor. Confidence can reinforce your message.
4. **Offer Alternatives:** If appropriate, suggest an alternative solution. For instance, if a friend invites you to a party but you cannot attend, you might say, "I can't come to the party, but let's hang out next weekend instead." This shows that you value the relationship while still prioritizing your needs.
5. **Practice Empathy:** Acknowledging feelings can soften the impact of your no. For example, you might say, "I understand this is important, but I can't take this on right now." This shows that you care while still standing by your decision.
6. **Stay Firm:** Once you say no, stick to it. It's okay to reiterate your no because it reinforces your boundaries.
7. **Practice Assertiveness:** Like any skill, assertive communication improves with practice. Role-playing different scenarios can help you feel more comfortable saying no assertively.

Mastering the art of saying no assertively is a game-changer. It empowers you to wade through diversified social situations with confidence and integrity, giving you the freedom to be authentic.

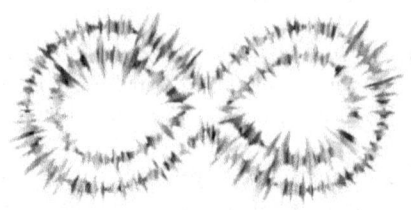

When to Walk Away

In life, we often face situations that make us feel uncomfortable, unhappy, or even unsafe. It is crucial to understand that we can walk away from a problem, whether it is a temporary challenge or a more permanent issue.

The concept of walking away dates back to ancient times when philosophers like Aristotle and Confucius discussed the importance of knowing when to leave a situation. They believed that walking away from conflict or negativity could lead to a more peaceful and fulfilling life.

Temporary situations to walk away from consist of circumstances that may have a negative impact on one's well-being or values. They are often short-lived challenges that may cause stress or discomfort but have the potential to improve with time.

Temporary circumstances could include relationships where you constantly feel undervalued, pressured to cooperate in risky behaviors, or your boundaries are being repeatedly crossed. Having the courage to step away from them allows individuals to prioritize their mental or emotional health.

Signs that it may be time to walk away from a temporary situation:
- **Negative Impact on Mental Health:** A situation is causing excessive stress, anxiety, or sadness
- **Lack of Personal Growth:** A situation is hindering your personal growth or prohibiting you from finishing your goals
- **Repeated Patterns:** You find yourself facing the same challenges repeatedly without any resolution

Walking away can be difficult, but there are certain situations where it is imperative to prioritize your well-being and safety by recognizing when it's time to leave for good. Unlike temporary situations, permanent ones are long-lasting challenges that may not quickly improve over time.

Permanent situations to walk away from include toxic relationships. Respect and kindness are lacking. Abusive environments harm your mental or physical health. Your values and beliefs are constantly compromised.

Identifying these permanent red flags will empower you to make decisions leading to a healthier and more fulfilling life. It's okay to prioritize your happiness and leave situations that do not serve you positively.

Signs that it may be time to walk away from a permanent situation:
- **Abusive Relationships:** Your safety and well-being are consistently endangered due to harmful environments
- **Unhealthy Work Conditions:** You repeatedly feel undervalued, overworked, or mistreated
- **Personal Values Compromised:** Your values or beliefs are continuously jeopardized

Walking away from a permanent situation can be challenging, but it is vital to prioritize your well-being and safety above all else. Keep in mind that you are not alone.

Whether you are facing a temporary or permanent situation, here are some tips:
1. **Create a Safety Plan:** If you are walking away from a dangerous or harmful situation, it is essential to create a safety plan to ensure your well-being during the transition.
2. **Set Boundaries:** When you decide to walk away, communicate this and set boundaries clearly. This action is a sign of self-respect and a way to protect yourself from negative influences.
3. **Focus on Self-Care:** Prioritize self-care activities such as exercise, meditation, or hobbies to help alleviate stress and promote overall well-being.
4. **Seek Support:** Talking to a qualified professional can help provide additional perspective and support during this challenging time.

Walking away from a situation does not mean giving up. It means prioritizing your well-being and happiness. Recognizing the signs that indicate it may be time to walk away empowers you to take control of your life. Create a healthier and more fulfilling future for yourself.

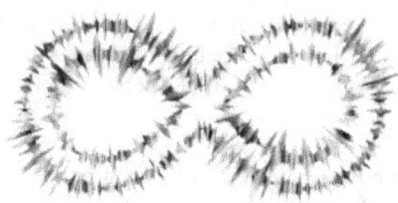

Responding To Abuse

Abuse can emerge in various forms, including physical, emotional, verbal, and even digital. Understanding that everyone has the right to be treated with respect and kindness is indispensable. If you are experiencing abuse in any way, it is essential to know when and how to walk away in a healthy manner. Walking away from abuse can be a challenging decision, but it is crucial for your well-being and safety.

The discovery of abuse can be traced back to ancient times when laws were established to protect individuals from violence. Abuse is a significant issue that can manifest in diverse ways. It's not always easy to identify and affects people of all ages, backgrounds, and genders.

Types of Abuse:
- **Physical abuse** relates to any form of violence or harm, such as the use of coercion that causes bodily injury, pain, or impairment. This category can inhabit numerous scenarios, including hitting, punching, kicking, burning, or any other action that causes harm to the body. It often results in visible marks or bruises on the victim's body, but it can also induce internal traumas that are not immediately apparent.
- **Mental or emotional abuse** can have long-term effects on a person's mental health and well-being. This type involves the manipulation, intimidation, and control of an individual through verbal or nonverbal actions. It can take the form of insults, threats, belittling, humiliation, or alienation, leading to feelings of fear, low self-esteem, and anxiety in the victim.
- **Sexual abuse** involves unwanted sexual activity or behavior. This type of abuse can include rape, molestation, unwanted touching, exposure to explicit materials, or any other sexual act performed without consent. It can have destructive repercussions on the victim's physical and emotional health, leading to feelings of shame, guilt, or confusion.

- **Neglect** refers to failing to provide the necessary care and support for basic needs. This can include not providing food, shelter, clothing, medical care, or emotional support. It can seriously disturb a person's health and well-being, leading to malnutrition, illness, poor hygiene, or emotional distress.
- **Financial abuse** consists of the misuse or withholding of a person's financial resources for the abuser's benefit. This can include stealing money or property, coercing someone to sign over their assets, or exploiting an individual's financial information for personal gain. It can leave the victim feeling powerless, insecure, and unable to meet their basic needs.
- **Digital abuse** refers to the misuse of technology to harass, intimidate, control, or bully another person. This can include spreading rumors online, sharing private information without consent, constantly monitoring someone's activities, or using social media to manipulate others.

Abuse can encompass numerous factors and can have severe consequences for the victims involved. Learning about the most common types enables us to work together to design a safer and more supportive environment for all members of our community.

Abuse is never acceptable. Do not justify being treated poorly under any circumstances. If you feel afraid, anxious, or unsafe around someone, it may be a sign of abuse. Trust your instincts. Pay attention to how you feel in the presence of the person causing harm. You have the right to feel safe and respected.

Red Flags:
- **Physical Violence:** This is one of the most recognizable forms of abusive behavior. It includes hitting, pushing, slapping, or any other physical actions that cause harm or injury to another person.
- **Verbal Abuse:** Constantly criticizing, insulting, belittling, or humiliating someone through words or tone of voice is a form of verbal abuse. This behavior can severely impact a person's self-esteem and mental well-being.
- **Controlling Behavior:** An abuser may try to control every aspect of their partner's life, including who they can see, what they can wear, or where they can go. This manipulative behavior can be a signal of an abusive relationship.
- **Isolation:** Abusers may try to isolate their victims from friends, family, or other support systems. This confinement makes it tough for the victim to reach out for help or escape from the abusive situation.
- **Gaslighting:** Gaslighting is a pattern of manipulation where the abuser makes the victim question their feelings, thoughts, or reality. It can be subtle but highly damaging to the victim's mental health.

- **Threats:** Making threats of harm, either towards the victim or themselves, is a serious red flag of abusive behavior. Threats can be used as a tool to control or intimidate the victim.
- **Jealousy and Possessiveness:** Excessive jealousy or possessiveness towards a partner can be indicative of abusive behavior. This standard of demeanor can lead to feelings of insecurity and fear in the relationship.

If the abusive behavior shows no sign of improvement despite addressing it with the person, it is crucial to prioritize your well-being and safety. Choosing to walk away from abuse is a courageous and empowering decision.

When you have decided to walk away from abuse, it is paramount to do so in a healthy and safe manner. If you recognize any red flags of abusive behavior in your relationships or someone else's, take action.

Steps to Take:
1. **Set Boundaries:** Clearly communicate your boundaries to the person exhibiting abusive behavior. Let them know that their actions are not acceptable.
2. **Safety Plan:** If you are in immediate danger, have a safety plan in place. This may include knowing who to call, where to go, and how to protect yourself.
3. **Talk to Someone:** Contact a trusted friend, family member, or counselor about your concerns.
4. **Seek Help:** If you feel unsafe or threatened, seek help from a counselor, therapist, or a local helpline specializing in domestic violence.

Your safety and well-being are the top priorities. Searching for help is not a sign of weakness. You deserve to be treated with respect and kindness at all times. If you are experiencing abuse, know that there are people who care about you and are ready to support you in walking away from harm. You are not alone. Help is available to guide you towards a life filled with love and respect.

If you do not know where to go for help, contact the National Domestic Violence Hotline. If you're in the United States, call 800.799.7233. Support is available 24 hours daily, seven days weekly, and 365 days yearly.

Leniency Towards Mistakes

Responses to mistakes or undesirable behaviors can vary significantly. It's important to distinguish between providing a safe space for growth and continuing abuse. During ancient Greece, philosophers such as Socrates and Aristotle discussed the importance of forgiveness as a virtue that promotes harmony and growth within communities. They emphasized that forgiving others for their mistakes can lead to personal and collective healing.

Everyone is prone to making mistakes. Leniency is like a warm embrace. It shows understanding, forgiveness, and patience towards individuals striving to rectify their errors.

Growth comes from accepting these mistakes and working towards betterment. When someone is lenient, they typically provide support, guidance, and constructive feedback to help the individual make corrections.

In a supportive environment, individuals feel encouraged to take risks, make mistakes, and learn from them without fearing severe consequences. This empowering approach focuses on the process of learning and development rather than solely on the end results.

The main difference between being lenient towards mistakes and not tolerating abuse lies in the intentions, outcomes, and impact on individuals. Leniency recognizes that making mistakes is a natural part of learning and values individuals' efforts to correct their behaviors. Abuse disregards the well-being of individuals, leading to a perpetuating cycle of pain, suffering, and emotional distress.

Concentrate on progress instead of perfection. Be lenient towards someone who is making genuine efforts to improve their behaviors.

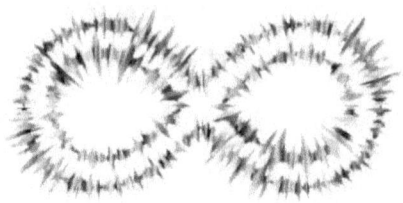

Moving Forward with Forgiveness

Forgiveness can bring healing and freedom to individuals who have experienced pain or trauma of any kind. Whether forgiving oneself for past mistakes or others who have caused harm, forgiveness can profoundly benefit one's mental, emotional, and even physical well-being.

One influential figure in the exploration of forgiveness is Mahatma Gandhi. He believed in the power of forgiveness as a means to achieve peace and justice. Gandhi said, "The weak can never forgive. Forgiveness is an attribute of the strong." His advocacy for nonviolent resistance and forgiveness inspired many others to seek reconciliation in times of conflict.

This journey involves consciously letting go of resentment, anger, or vengeance towards someone who wronged us. It does not mean we condone or excuse the hurtful actions of others.

We can release ourselves from the heavy emotional burdens that weigh us down. This path of forgiveness can take time and effort, but the rewards are invaluable.

Impact of Forgiving Oneself:
- When we forgive ourselves for past faults or shortcomings, we choose to break free from self-imposed guilt and shame. Acknowledging our imperfections and showing self-compassion empowers us to develop a sense of self-acceptance and inner peace. Forgiving ourselves allows us to learn from our experiences, grow more robust, and move forward with a renewed sense of self-worth and confidence.

Impact of Forgiving Others:
- Forgiving those who have hurt us can be a challenging and transformative experience. Choosing to forgive releases the burden of carrying anger and resentment toward the other person. This does not mean that we forget what happened or reconcile with the individual.

- In forgiving others, we choose to let go of the negative emotions that can hold us back. Forgiveness can sometimes lead to increased empathy, understanding, and even reconciliation. It can also help us break the cycle of hurt and pain, allowing us to move forward with peace and closure.

Impact of Forgiveness in Abusive Situations:
- In cases of abusive relationships, forgiveness can offer a pivotal purpose in the healing and recovery process. While it is imperative to prioritize safety and seek help when in abusive situations, forgiving oneself for staying in the relationship or forgiving the abuser can be a potent step towards reclaiming one's sense of agency.
- Forgiveness can help survivors of abuse break free from the cycle of victimhood and reclaim their power. It can also lead to a sense of empowerment, allowing individuals to let go of the pain or trauma of the past and embrace a brighter future.

Overall Wellness Benefits:
1. **Mental and Emotional Healing:** Forgiveness grants individuals liberation from unfavorable emotions that hold them back from moving forward. It can reduce feelings of anger, resentment, and guilt.
2. **Improved Relationships:** Forgiveness is about building healthier connections. It's about practicing trust and understanding. This creates a more harmonious and fulfilling relationship with ourselves and others.
3. **Release from Painful Memories:** Forgiveness can help individuals break free from the burden of past experiences. It allows them to focus on the present moment and the future.
4. **Personal Growth:** Forgiveness permits individuals to gain wisdom from their experiences, develop resilience, and move forward with renewed strength and determination.
5. **Inner Peace:** Letting go of past experiences enables individuals to find peace within themselves. This peace is a deep sense of calm, acceptance, and contentment. Forgiveness can create a brighter future for individuals who practice it.

Embracing forgiveness can help you release counterproductive thoughts and feelings. Embarking on this journey offers healing and a renewed hope for the future.

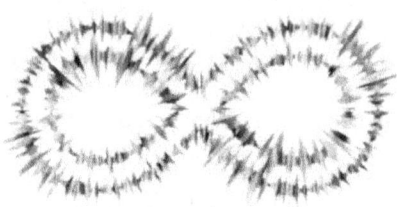

Loving Deeply

Love is a complex and powerful emotion that can manifest in many ways. Someone who loves deeply may give their all to a relationship or connection with another person. Loving passionately does not equate to being desperate.

Love was often intertwined with myths and legends in ancient cultures such as Mesopotamia, Egypt, Greece, and Rome. The Greeks, for example, had multiple words to describe different types of love, including "agape" for unconditional love and "eros" for romantic love. The famous Greek philosopher Plato explored the idea of love in his dialogues, emphasizing this complex emotion's spiritual and intellectual aspects.

Loving hard without being desperate means enacting self-love practices. When you value and respect yourself, you might find that you no longer need to seek validation from your partner or others constantly.

Instead, you recognize your worth, have confidence in yourself, and don't depend on someone else to complete you. This self-assurance forms the foundation for healthy relationships, allowing you to love others deeply without losing yourself in the process.

Healthy relationships are built on vulnerable and truthful communication where both parties feel heard and understood. When someone experiences interdependence, they are willing to confess their thoughts, feelings, and needs to their partner without fear of rejection or judgment. Clear and respectful communication enables individuals to love passionately while maintaining self-care.

Boundaries define the limits of a relationship and help ensure that both individuals' needs are respected. Without boundaries, you might find yourself constantly sacrificing your needs and values for the sake of the relationship.

Trust is the foundation of any healthy connection. It lets individuals feel secure in their partner's feelings and intentions. When someone loves deeply but trusts their partner and the relationship's stability, they can express their love authentically without resorting to desperate behaviors. Trusting in their bond enables individuals to love passionately while maintaining a sense of security and emotional balance.

Self-neglect can prompt feelings of resentment and a loss of self-identity. Prioritize your well-being. Know when to say no. Do not compromise your values for the sake of any relationship.

Strike a balance between passion, self-respect, intensity, and independence. Embrace mutual respect, support, and understanding, where individuals grow and flourish together.

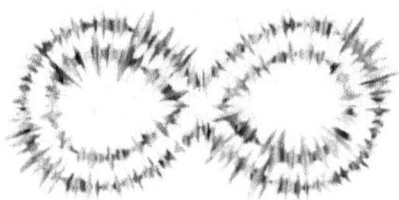

Self-Neglect

Self-neglect is the act of neglecting one's own needs for care, support, and well-being. It can manifest in various ways, such as overlooking personal hygiene, avoiding medical care, or failing to meet basic nutritional needs.

One of the early pioneers in the study of self-neglect was Dr. Eleanor Silverberg, a renowned psychologist who led extensive research on the topic in the mid-20th century. Dr. Silverberg's work focused on understanding why some individuals fail to care for themselves despite being capable of doing so. Through her research, she identified various underlying causes of self-neglect, including mental health issues, trauma, and social isolation.

When individuals engage in self-neglect, it can disrupt their ability to process their thoughts and emotions. It can also create barriers to effective self-communication by undermining one's sense of self-worth.

Neglecting their basic needs can lead to feelings of imperfection and worthlessness. As a result, they may struggle to engage in positive self-talk, which is essential for maintaining a healthy self-image.

They may become disconnected from their inner experiences. This detachment can make it challenging to make sense of one's emotions, leading to increased anxiety, stress, and emotional turmoil.

Make sure to reserve time for self-care. Addressing self-neglect provides hope and motivation for our self-love journey.

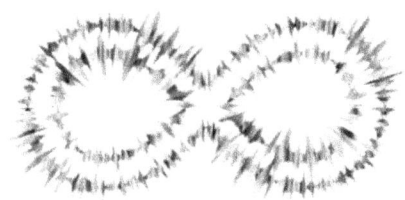

Smart Goals

One of the best ways to improve self-care is by setting smart goals. Applying these principles can help you clarify your thoughts, stay focused, and achieve your objectives. George T. Doran first introduced the smart goals framework in 1981. He aimed to help managers and organizations create more effective and achievable goals. He recognized that many goals were often too vague, leading to confusion about expectations and outcomes.

Details for Each Component:
- **Specific goals** are clear and well-defined. Instead of saying, "I want to get better at math," it can be altered to, "I want to improve my math grade from a C to a B."
- **Measurable goals** help you track your progress. For example, instead of "I want to read more books," you could set a goal to "read one book per month."
- **Achievable goals** are realistic and attainable. Set goals that challenge you but are still possible. For instance, if you have a busy schedule, instead of aiming to study three hours a day, you might set a goal to study for 30 minutes each day.
- **Relevant goals** are meaningful to you. It should align with your values and long-term objectives. If you want to pursue a career in science, a relevant goal could be "I will join the science club to enhance my knowledge and experiences."
- **Time-bound goals** have a deadline. This helps you stay focused and motivated. Instead of saying, "I want to learn to play the guitar," a time-bound goal would be, "I want to learn three songs on the guitar by the end of the semester."

Tips:
1. **Reflect on Your Goals:** Take some time to think about what you want to achieve. This could be related to academics, sports, personal interests, or relationships. Write down your thoughts and feelings. Reflecting on your goals helps you understand what is truly important to you.

2. **Create Your Goals:** Once you have a list of potential goals, turn them into smart goals. Ask yourself the following questions for each goal:
   - Is it specific? Can I clearly define what I want to achieve?
   - How will I measure my progress?
   - Is this goal achievable within my current circumstances?
   - Does this goal align with my values and long-term plans?
   - What is my deadline for achieving this goal?
3. **Record Your Goals:** Write down your goals to solidify your commitment. Keep them visible, perhaps on a poster in your room or a planner. Doing so can serve as a constant reminder of what you are working towards.
4. **Develop a Plan of Action:** Creating a plan of action is crucial for achieving your goals. Break your goals into smaller, manageable tasks. For example, if your goal is to read one book per month, you could set a goal to read ten pages daily. This makes the goal less overwhelming and helps you stay on track.
5. **Monitor Your Progress:** Regularly check your progress toward your goals. This is where the "measurable" aspect comes into play. You can utilize a journal, calendar, or apps to track your achievements. Monitoring your progress allows you to celebrate small victories and make adjustments if needed.
6. **Reflect and Adjust:** Periodically reflect on your goals and progress. Are you still committed to them? Do they still feel relevant? If not, it's okay to adjust them or set new goals. Flexibility ensures that your goals continue to reflect your interests and aspirations.

Using smart goals helps you clarify your objectives and stay focused on what matters most. Smart goals are an effective tool to guide you on your journey. Set your goals and watch how your life transforms.

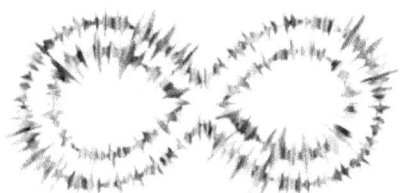

Fundamental Life Skills

Life is filled with challenges. With the correct set of skills, we can successfully navigate uncertainties. These interconnected skills contribute to our overall personal growth and success. The notion of fundamental life skills can be traced back to ancient philosophers who accentuated the importance of acquiring knowledge and skills beyond academic subjects.

One of the earliest proponents for success in life was taught by Aristotle. He believed education should focus on intellectual pursuits and developing practical skills crucial for a fulfilling life.

Ten Fundamental Life Skills:
1. **Communication Skills:** Communication is indispensable in every aspect of life. Communicating effectively can help you build strong relationships, succeed in your endeavors, and avoid misunderstandings.
2. **Critical Thinking:** Critical thinking involves analyzing information, evaluating arguments, and problem-solving. Developing this skill can help you make sound decisions, think creatively, and approach challenges rationally.
3. **Emotional Intelligence:** Comprehending and managing your emotions is essential for your mental well-being and relationships with others. Emotional intelligence involves self-regulation and empathy that can help you navigate various social situations successfully.
4. **Time Management:** Learning to manage your time efficiently is central to achieving your goals and reducing stress. Effective time management involves setting priorities, creating schedules, and avoiding procrastination.
5. **Financial Literacy:** Understanding basic financial concepts like budgeting, saving, and managing money is paramount for long-term financial stability. Developing financial literacy can help you make informed decisions to secure your future.

6. **Resilience:** Life is like a rollercoaster full of ups and downs. Resilience is what helps you bounce back from setbacks and challenges. Developing resilience involves cultivating a positive mindset, adapting to change, and learning from failures.
7. **Adaptability:** Adaptability is essential in a rapidly changing world. Adaptability involves being open to new experiences, learning from feedback, and adjusting to different situations.
8. **Leadership Skills:** Even if you're not in a formal leadership position, having leadership skills such as teamwork, decisiveness, or problem-solving can help you influence others positively, take action, and work well in group settings.
9. **Conflict Resolution:** Conflict is a natural part of life, but knowing how to resolve conflicts peacefully and constructively is a valuable skill. Effective communication, empathy, and negotiation can help you resolve conflicts with friends, family, and colleagues.
10. **Self-Care:** Caring for yourself is vital for your mind, body, and soul. Practicing self-care activities like exercise, mindfulness, and relaxation can help you recharge, reduce stress, and improve your quality of life.

This lifelong journey requires practice, patience, and a growth mindset. With effort and determination, you can acquire the tools you need to thrive in all areas of your life.

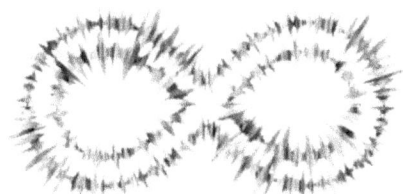

Emotional Intelligence

Psychologists Peter Salovey and John Mayer first recognized emotional intelligence in the early 1990s. However, its roots can be traced back to the work of psychologists and researchers who explored the role of emotions in human behavior long before Salovey and Mayer.

Emotional intelligence encompasses the capability to recognize, understand, and manage our emotions effectively. It influences how we interpret and respond to the world around us.

Four Main Components:
1. **Self-awareness** involves understanding our emotions, including recognizing how they affect our thoughts and behavior.
2. **Self-management** allows us to regulate and control our emotions in various situations. This includes managing stress, impulses, and reactions.
3. **Social awareness** means understanding the emotions and needs of others.
4. **Relationship management** involves effectively managing interpersonal relationships using empathy, communication skills, and conflict resolution techniques.

Impact:
- **Misunderstanding Emotions:** One of the primary impacts of poor emotional intelligence is the inability to understand and interpret our emotions. When we don't recognize our feelings, it becomes challenging to express them accurately. For instance, if a student feels anxious about a presentation but cannot identify that feeling, they might communicate their discomfort in an unclear or aggressive manner. This can confuse friends and classmates, leading to further anxiety and misinterpretations.

- **Difficulty Expressing Needs:** Good emotional intelligence helps us articulate our needs and desires effectively. Without it, we may struggle to ask for help or express our needs to others. For example, a student who feels overwhelmed with homework might not know how to communicate their feelings to a teacher or parent. Instead of expressing their need for assistance, they might remain silent or complain, which does not lead to a resolution. This can lead to feelings of frustration, making it harder to cope with challenges.
- **Increased Conflict:** Poor emotional intelligence often leads to misunderstandings and conflicts in communication. When we cannot recognize our emotions or those of others, we may react impulsively or defensively. For instance, if a friend makes a joke that we perceive as hurtful, a lack of emotional understanding might cause us to respond angrily instead of discussing our feelings. This can escalate into a conflict that could have been avoided with clear and empathetic communication.
- **Negative Self-Talk:** Self-communication also includes how we talk to ourselves. Poor emotional intelligence can lead to negative self-talk, which affects our self-esteem and motivation. For example, if a student receives a low grade, they might think, "I'm not good enough," instead of recognizing the situation as a chance to learn and improve. This cycle can hinder their ability to communicate effectively with themselves and others, leading to a lack of confidence in expressing thoughts and feelings.
- **Difficulty Building Relationships:** Emotional intelligence is critical to forming and maintaining healthy relationships. When we struggle with self-communication due to low emotional intelligence, it can be challenging to connect with others. For instance, if a student does not know how to express disappointment, they might withdraw from friends instead of talking about their feelings. This withdrawal can lead to misunderstandings and distance in relationships, making it difficult to foster meaningful connections with peers.
- **Complications with Conflict Resolution:** Conflict resolution is an essential skill that relies heavily on emotional intelligence. When individuals cannot understand their emotions or those of others, resolving disputes becomes more complicated. For example, during a disagreement, a student who cannot articulate their feelings may resort to avoidance or aggression instead of seeking a compromise. This can lead to unresolved issues and lingering resentment, further complicating relationships.

Benefits:
- **Self-Reflection:** Individuals with high emotional intelligence can objectively analyze their strengths, weaknesses, and areas for growth without harsh criticism.

- **Emotional Regulation:** Those with high emotional intelligence can navigate challenging situations without becoming overwhelmed by their feelings.
- **Positive Self-Talk:** People with high emotional intelligence tend to practice boosting self-esteem and resilience.
- **Conflict Resolution:** Approaching inner conflicts with empathy and understanding enables us to constructively work towards resolution and personal growth.

Tips:
1. **Mindfulness:** Meditation or deep breathing can help increase self-awareness and emotional regulation.
2. **Journaling:** Keeping a record of thoughts and emotions can aid in identifying patterns and triggers.
3. **Empathy Building:** Engaging in acts of kindness or empathy towards others can enhance our social awareness and empathy towards ourselves.
4. **Seeking Feedback:** Establish a trusting relationship with a qualified individual to ensure you receive reliable support and advice.

Emotional intelligence provides a transformative force. Honing these skills allows individuals to establish a healthier relationship with themselves, improve mental well-being, and navigate life's challenges with resilience and compassion.

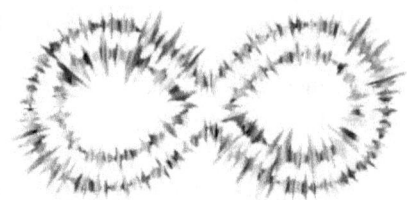

Time Management

Time is of the essence. In the hustle and bustle of our intricate lives, effective time management can influence how we talk to ourselves, set goals, make decisions, and manage stress. One of the earliest known figures to emphasize the importance of time management was the ancient Greek philosopher Aristotle. In his work, he discussed the significance of time and how it can be used wisely to achieve success.

Impact:
- When individuals do not manage their time well, they may be overwhelmed with tasks. This can cloud their ability to think clearly. Instead of encouraging ourselves, we might engage in negative self-talk like, "I'm never going to get this done," or "I can't handle this pressure." This kind of thinking can harm our self-esteem and make it even harder to manage our time effectively.
- When deadlines are missed, and responsibilities pile up, individuals may feel a sense of panic. This can lead to a cycle in which the pressure of managing time causes even more stress, making it difficult to focus on tasks. We may fail to listen to our inner voice or ignore our needs when stressed.
- When we rush through tasks or leave things until the last minute, we are less likely to think critically about our choices. This can lead to mistakes. For instance, if a student waits until the night before a big exam to study, they may not perform well and then tell themselves, "I'm just not good at this subject." This can lead to decreased confidence.

Benefits:
- **Reduce Stress:** You can avoid rushing when you manage your time well. Planning allows you to feel more in control of your tasks.

Time Management

- **Improve Productivity:** Effective time management allows you to accomplish more in less time. This means you can be more productive during your study sessions and free up time for other activities.
- **Enhance Self-Discipline:** As you practice this skill, you will find that you are also more disciplined in other areas of your life.

Tips:
1. **Practice Positive Self-Talk:** Reframe negative thoughts with positive affirmations. Remind yourself of your strengths and successes to boost confidence.
2. **Set Clear Goals:** Identify what you want to achieve. Break larger tasks into smaller steps to make progress more manageable. Use the smart criteria for your goals.
    - **Specific:** Define your goals clearly (e.g., "I want to finish my math homework by Thursday").
    - **Measurable:** Measure your progress (e.g., "I will complete three math problems each day").
    - **Achievable:** Ensure your goals are realistic (e.g., "I will study for my math test for 30 minutes each day").
    - **Relevant:** Your goals should align with your objectives (e.g., "I want to improve my math grade").
    - **Time-bound:** Set a deadline for your goals (e.g., "I will complete my project by the end of the week").
3. **Create a Schedule:** It can help you organize your time effectively. Use a planner, calendar, or even a digital app to keep track of your tasks, deadlines, and appointments. This helps visualize what needs to be done and when.
    - **List Your Tasks:** Write down everything you need to do for the week, including homework, projects, and personal responsibilities.
    - **Prioritize Tasks:** Highlight the most important or time-sensitive tasks. Focus on completing these tasks first.
    - **Set Time Limits:** Allocate time slots for each task. This will prevent you from spending too much time on one activity, reduce stress, and allow for clearer thinking.
4. **Use Time Blocks:** Time blocking is a technique that dedicates specific chunks of time to different activities. For example, set aside 6 PM to 7 PM for homework and 7 PM to 8 PM for leisure activities. Time blocks allow you to create a structured approach to your day, which makes it easier to stay on track.
5. **Eliminate Distractions:** They can eat away at your time and hinder your productivity. Identify what distracts you most, whether it's your phone, social media, or television. Create a dedicated workspace free from distractions to help you focus better.

6. **Take Breaks:** Regular breaks can enhance your productivity. Working long periods without a break can lead to burnout and decreased focus. Try the Pomodoro Technique. This is where you work for 25 minutes. Then, you take a 5-minute break. Once you complete four rotations, take a longer break, such as 15-30 minutes. It can help you stay refreshed and maintain your focus.
7. **Reflect and Adjust:** At the end of each week, take some time to reflect on how well you managed your time. Did you accomplish your goals? What worked well, and what didn't? Use this reflection to adjust your strategies for the following week. Flexibility is key. If something isn't working, try a different approach. This can help you understand your feelings and improve your communication.

Work smarter, not harder. Instead of rushing to complete tasks at the last minute, allocate your time more efficiently. This way, you can complete your work on time and have time left over for leisure activities.

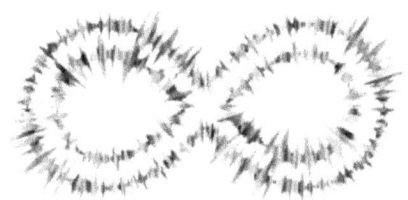

Financial Literacy

Financial literacy encompasses the knowledge and application of concepts such as budgeting, saving, investing, and money management. The idea of financial literacy dates back to ancient civilizations where basic economic principles were taught to ensure the prosperity of communities.

In early Mesopotamia, clay tablets were used to record financial transactions, demonstrating an early form of financial record-keeping. As societies evolved, the need for financial knowledge became more apparent, laying the foundation for the modern concept of financial literacy.

Impact:

- **Inability to Express Needs:** Individuals lacking financial literacy may struggle to articulate their monetary needs. For example, if someone does not understand how much they can afford to spend, they may hesitate to ask for help or advice from others. This can lead to frustration.
- **Fear of Judgment:** Those with limited financial knowledge may fear being judged by others. They might worry that friends or family will think less of them if they admit they struggle financially. This can prevent them from opening up about their financial issues, which can be detrimental to their mental health and relationships.
- **Difficulty Setting Goals:** People without strong financial literacy skills may struggle to set realistic financial goals. Without a clear understanding of what they can achieve, they may not communicate their aspirations effectively, leading to confusion and dissatisfaction.
- **Misunderstanding Financial Terms:** Many financial discussions involve specific terminology, such as "interest rates," "credit scores," and "investment returns." Individuals who do not understand these terms may find engaging in conversations about their finances difficult. This misunderstanding can make them feel unconfident and less likely to participate.

- **Poor Decision-Making:** When someone lacks these skills, they may make impulsive financial decisions based on emotions rather than logic. Poor decision-making can lead to adverse outcomes, such as taking on debt, which can be hard to communicate. When individuals cannot explain their choices or the consequences, they may feel overwhelmed and unable to seek advice from others.

Benefits:
- **Better Money Management:** One of the most significant benefits of financial literacy is better money management. You can track your income and expenses when financially literate. This helps you prioritize your spending. For example, if you receive an allowance or earn money from a part-time job, knowing how to allocate your funds can help you save for the things you want, such as a new video game or a special outing with friends.
- **Savings and Emergency Funds:** Good financial literacy skills encourage the habit of saving. When you understand the importance of saving, you can set aside money for future needs or emergencies. An emergency fund provides security in unexpected situations, such as medical expenses or car repairs.
- **Understanding Credit and Debt:** Many people rely on credit cards or loans to make purchases. Without knowledge of how these work, you can easily fall into debt.

    For example, knowing how interest affects the total cost over time is crucial if you want to buy a car and need a loan. You will pay back more than just the original amount. Understanding this can help you make better borrowing decisions and avoid excessive debt.
- **Investing for the Future:** Investing means using your money to earn more money over time. This can be done through stocks, bonds, or real estate. Although investing may seem complicated, understanding the basics can lead to significant financial growth.

    Starting early with investments can lead to substantial benefits in the long run. For instance, if you invest $100 a month starting at age 15, you could have a substantial amount saved by the time you reach retirement age, thanks to compound interest. Understanding how investments work can motivate you to save early and choose the suitable options.
- **Making Informed Decisions:** Knowledge helps you weigh your options, whether choosing a bank account, selecting an insurance plan, or deciding whether to buy or rent.

    For example, understanding the fees, interest rates, and benefits can help you choose the correct bank account. You can ask the right questions and avoid pitfalls that could cost you money in the long run.

- **Building Confidence and Independence:** Good financial literacy skills build confidence and independence. When you understand how to manage your finances, you feel more in control of your life.

Tips:
1. **Start with the Basics:**
   - **Income:** The money you earn from work, investments, or other sources.
   - **Expenses:** The money you spend on necessities like food, housing, and transportation.
   - **Savings:** The portion of your income you set aside for future use.
   - **Debt:** Money you owe others, often due to loans or credit card purchases.
2. **Create a Budget:** You can see where your money goes and make adjustments to save more effectively.
   - **List Your Income:** Write down all money sources you receive each month.
   - **Track Your Expenses:** Keep a record of all your spending. This can be done using apps or a simple spreadsheet. Categorize your expenses into needs and wants.
   - **Set Spending Limits:** Decide how much money you can spend in different categories.
   - **Review Regularly:** Check your budget every month. Ensure you stay on track by adjusting it as needed.
3. **Learn about Saving and Investing:** Start with simple goals. For instance, you might aim to save a portion of your weekly income. Even small amounts can add up over time. Saving early helps you be better prepared for larger financial responsibilities in the future.
   - **Set Savings Goals:** Determine your objective, whether it's a new phone, a car, or a home. Specific goals make it easier to stay motivated.
   - **Open a Savings Account:** Keep your money safe while earning interest in a savings account.
   - **Understand Investment Options:** Learn about different types of investments, including stocks, bonds, and mutual funds. Each has its risks and potential rewards.
4. **Use Financial Education Resources:**
   - **Books:** Look for books focused on personal finance.
   - **Online Courses:** Websites like Khan Academy and Coursera offer free courses on personal finance topics. These can give you a deeper understanding of financial concepts.
   - **Podcasts and Videos:** Many financial experts share their knowledge through podcasts and YouTube channels. These can be a fun way to learn while multitasking.
5. **Practice Real-Life Financial Decisions:**

- **Manage Your Money:** If you earn money doing something, practice budgeting and saving with that money.
- **Simulate Investments:** Use online simulators to practice buying and selling stocks without using real money. This can help you understand how the stock market works.
- **Plan a Small Project:** Try setting a budget for a small project, like a birthday party or an event. This will give you hands-on experience managing money.

6. **Seek Guidance from Financial Advisers:** Don't hesitate to ask for help when learning about finances. Financial advisers can clarify concepts and offer advice on various financial matters. Having a mentor can make the learning process smoother and more enjoyable.
7. **Stay Informed about Financial News:** Finally, staying updated on financial news can enhance your understanding of the economy and personal finance. Follow reputable news sources, and read articles or watch videos that cover financial topics. Learning about current events can help you understand how monetary systems work and how they affect your finances.

Financial proficiency is the key to unlocking the power of financial control. Individuals with high financial literacy are better equipped to navigate the world's complexities and make sound financial choices.

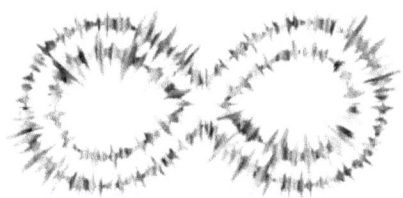

Resilience

Resilience is the capability to bounce back from challenges and setbacks. One of the earliest known references to resilience comes from the Stoic philosophers in the early 3rd century BCE.

Impact:
- **Mental Health Consequences:** When individuals encounter stress or adversity, a lack of resilience can lead to feelings of helplessness and hopelessness. This can cause anxiety and depression, making it difficult for someone to enjoy life or feel motivated. People may experience headaches, fatigue, or stomach issues.
- **Academic Performance:** Without resilience, individuals may avoid challenges, fearing failure or disappointment. This lack of effort can lead to poor grades, diminishing their confidence and motivation. Over time, this can create a pattern of underachievement, where they become disengaged and disinterested in their studies.

  Additionally, people lacking resilience may struggle to manage their time effectively, leading to procrastination. They may feel overwhelmed by deadlines, resulting in rushed work and missed learning opportunities. This can create a cycle of frustration that affects their self-esteem.
- **Impact on Relationships:** Individuals lacking resilience may withdraw from friends and family during tough times. They might feel embarrassed or ashamed to share their struggles, which can result in loneliness and damage to relationships over time.

  A lack of resilience can lead to misunderstandings and conflicts in relationships. Less resilient people might react more intensely to disagreements or criticism, leading to arguments. They may struggle to see the other person's perspective, causing further strain in friendships or family dynamics.

- **Overall Well-being:** The long-term effects of not being resilient can significantly impact overall well-being. Emotional well-being is closely tied to resilience. Without it, individuals may struggle to find joy in everyday activities. They may feel stuck and unable to move forward or pursue their goals.

    Chronic stress from not coping well with challenges weakens the immune system. It can make them more susceptible to illnesses.

Resilient people tend to have a more positive and empowering inner voice when faced with difficulties. Instead of being overly critical or defeatist, they are more likely to offer themselves encouragement, support, and constructive feedback.

For instance, instead of saying, 'I can't do this,' they might say, 'I can do this. I've overcome challenges before.' This optimistic self-talk can boost confidence, motivation, and mental strength, forming the foundation for effective self-communication.

Individuals with high levels of flexibility are better equipped to maintain a healthy self-image even during adversity. They are more likely to view hardships as opportunities for growth rather than insurmountable obstacles. This positive self-perception enables them to foster a sense of inner stability and confidence.

Resilient individuals are better equipped to navigate stress, uncertainty, and setbacks without spiraling into negativity or despair. Maintaining a resilient mindset helps you prioritize self-care, seek social support, and adapt to challenges. This proactive approach to well-being nurtures a supportive and compassionate communication style with oneself.

Tips:
1. **Develop Self-Awareness:** Become more aware of your thoughts, emotions, and reactions to challenging situations. Recognize when negative self-talk creeps in and practice replacing it with more constructive and affirming messages.
2. **Practice Mindfulness:** Engage in meditation, deep breathing, or yoga to manage stress more effectively. Mindfulness can help you examine your thoughts and respond to them with compassion.
3. **Set Realistic Goals:** Break down larger goals into smaller steps to build confidence and motivation. Acknowledge your resilience in overcoming obstacles. Celebrate your successes along the way. This practice promotes a positive self-perception.
4. **Build a Support Network:** Seek support from a qualified professional, such as a psychiatrist or a life coach, that you can trust.

Empower yourself through resilience. Let it guide you to face challenges with courage, adaptability, and a growth-oriented mindset.

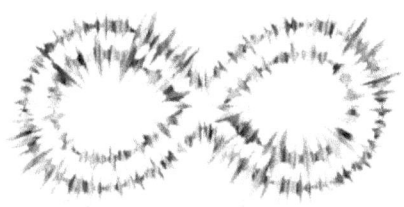

Adaptability

Adaptability refers to the capability to adjust one's behavior to thrive in different environments. The concept of adaptability can be traced back to the work of Charles Darwin, a renowned naturalist and biologist.

In the 19th century, Darwin proposed the theory of evolution through natural selection, which radically altered our understanding of how species change over time. His observations led him to conclude that organisms adapt to their surroundings through natural selection.

Impact:

- **Emotional Consequences:** When people cannot adapt to new situations, they may experience various emotional difficulties. One of the most common issues is increased stress. Not being adaptable can result in a fixed mindset.

  When individuals believe they cannot change or grow, they may avoid challenges and give up easily. This mindset can be detrimental to their self-esteem because they may feel inadequate when facing difficulties.

- **Social Implications:** The inability to adapt can also affect relationships with others. Social interactions often require flexibility and understanding.

  If a group member is unwilling to compromise or adjust their ideas, it can lead to conflicts and hinder the group's success. Reluctance to change can create distance in friendships and lead to loneliness.

- **Academic Challenges:** Adaptability is vital for success. Those who resist change may find it challenging to keep up with new material or expectations. If students are unwilling to try new things or step outside their comfort zone, they may miss opportunities to develop new skills, discover new interests, or meet new friends.

Tips:
1. **Embrace a Growth Mindset:** View change as an opportunity for growth rather than a threat. When faced with new situations, remind yourself that adapting can lead to new experiences and learning.
   - **Reframe Your Beliefs:** Instead of thinking, "I can't do this," try saying, "I can learn how to do this." This simple change in thought can motivate you to tackle challenges.
   - **Learn from Failure:** Failure is a part of the learning process. When something doesn't go as planned, reflect on your experience and how to improve next time.
   - **Set Smart Goals:** Start with small, achievable goals that require stepping out of your comfort zone. Gradually increase the complexity of these goals as you become more comfortable with change. This helps you focus on progress rather than perfection.
2. **Stay Informed:** The more you know about the world around you, the easier it is to adjust to changes.
   - **Read Widely:** Explore books, articles, and news from various fields. This will provide different perspectives on situations.
   - **Engage in Discussions:** Talk with friends, family, and classmates about current events and ideas. Engaging in discussions helps you understand different viewpoints and enhances your critical thinking skills.
   - **Stay Open to New Experiences:** Try new activities, join clubs, or attend workshops. Experiencing new things helps you learn to adjust to different environments and challenges.
3. **Practice Problem-Solving Skills:** When challenges arise, take a step back and analyze the situation. Consider different solutions and be willing to try various approaches.
   - **Identify the Problem:** Clearly define what the challenge is. Understanding the problem is the first step to finding a solution.
   - **Brainstorm Solutions:** Write down all possible solutions. The goal is to generate as many ideas as possible.
   - **Evaluate Options:** Look at your list of solutions. Weigh the pros and cons of each. Choose the best option based on your evaluation.
   - **Take Action:** Implement your chosen solution and monitor the results. If it doesn't work, try another approach.
4. **Develop Emotional Intelligence:** Keep an open mind when encountering new ideas or perspectives. Listen to others and be willing to consider their viewpoints.
   - **Self-Reflection:** Take time to reflect on your emotions and reactions to different situations. This will help you manage them better.

Adaptability

- **Practice Empathy:** Understanding things from other people's perspectives can improve your relationships and make you more adaptable in social situations.
- **Stay Calm Under Pressure:** Learn techniques to manage stress, such as deep breathing or mindfulness. Remaining tranquil allows clear thinking while faced with challenges.

5. **Build a Support Network:** A robust support system can significantly enhance adaptability. Friends, family, teachers, and mentors can provide encouragement and guidance.
   - **Connect with Others:** Make an effort to build relationships. Networking can lead to new opportunities and support in times of change.
   - **Share Experiences:** Discussing challenges with others can lead to new ideas and solutions. Sharing your experiences can also help others in similar situations.
   - **Seek Feedback:** Ask people you trust about how you handle change. Use this feedback to improve your adaptability skills.

Being open to change permits individuals to engage in a more meaningful, insightful, and constructive inner dialogue. It empowers individuals to navigate life's challenges with confidence.

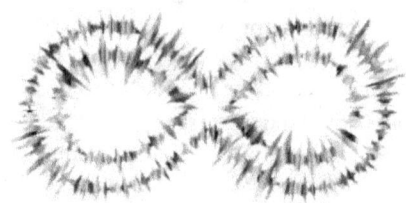

Enacting Self-Love

Love is a universal language we all speak, but did you know we each have a unique way of expressing and feeling loved? Dr. Gary Chapman discusses five primary ways people display and accept love in his 1992 publication "The 5 Love Languages."

Engaging in these love languages triggers the release of feel-good hormones, such as oxytocin, dopamine, endorphins, and serotonin. When you find yourself on the receiving end of a love language, it's crucial to reflect, "How would I feel if someone rejected one of my primary love languages?" This understanding enables us to communicate our affection more effectively, strengthening our relationships with ourselves and others.

The 5 Love Languages:
1. **Physical touch** emphasizes the importance of physical affection. To practice self-love, find ways to give yourself comforting physical sensations.

    Tips for Physical Touch:
    - **Massage:** Take time to allow yourself a professional massage. Doing so can relieve tension and promote relaxation.
    - **Warm Baths:** Make yourself a warm bath with soothing scents. This can be a great way to unwind and pamper yourself.
    - **Cuddle with a Pet:** If you have a pet, spend time cuddling with them. The physical connection can boost your mood and increase feelings of happiness.
2. **Quality time** is about spending time with yourself in a meaningful way. It means being present and engaged in what you are doing.

    Tips for Quality Time:
    - **Mindfulness Practices:** Engage in meditation, yoga, or sitting quietly with your thoughts. This helps you connect with yourself on a deeper level.

- **Pursue Hobbies:** Dedicate time to hobbies that you love. Whether painting, playing an instrument, or gardening, investing time in enjoyable activities can be very rewarding.
- **Solo Adventures:** Plan a day to explore a new place, hike, or visit a museum. Enjoying your own company can enhance your sense of self-worth.

3. **Words of affirmation** refer to expressing love through verbal encouragement, praise, and compliments. Hearing kind words can boost self-esteem and promote a positive self-image for many.

    Tips for Words of Affirmation:
    - **Positive Self-Talk:** Start each day by telling yourself positive affirmations. For example, say, "I am capable," or "I am worthy of love." Write these affirmations down and read them aloud to make them even more powerful.
    - **Journaling:** Keep a journal of your achievements, qualities, and things you love about yourself. Reviewing these entries can remind you of your worth.
    - **Verbal Praise:** When you accomplish something, no matter how small, celebrate that success with kind words.

4. **Acts of service** involve doing something helpful for others, but you can apply this love language to yourself. You can care for your physical, emotional, and mental well-being.

    Tips for Acts of Service:
    - **Self-Care Routine:** Develop a regimen that includes activities you enjoy, such as cooking, walking, or meditating.
    - **Set Boundaries:** Say no to things that drain your energy. Prioritize your time and energy towards things that revitalize you.
    - **Organize Your Space:** Take time to declutter and organize your living or working space. A clean atmosphere can lead to a clearer mind.

5. **Gifting** is not just about receiving material items. It can also mean giving yourself thoughtful gifts that show you care.

    Tips for Gifting:
    - **Treat Yourself:** Occasionally buy yourself something special, whether it's a favorite snack, a new book, or a fun activity. This shows that you value yourself.
    - **Create a "Self-Gift" List:** Make a list of things you would like to treat yourself to, such as a movie night or a day at the spa. Set aside time to make these gifts a reality.

- **Celebrate Milestones:** Acknowledge and celebrate your achievements with a small gift to yourself. This could be a day off to do something you love or a small item that brings you joy.

Self-love is not selfish. It is essential for happiness and well-being. Practice these love languages regularly to notice a positive change in how you feel about yourself.

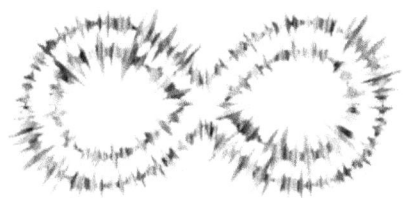

Feel, Felt, Found

The "feel, felt, found" method is an extraordinary technique that empowers you to express yourself more clearly. It's a convenient tool that can guide you through dealing with difficult emotions and navigating complex situations, putting you in control of your emotional journey.

The concept of feel, felt, found was popularized by Dale Carnegie, an influential writer on self-improvement and interpersonal skills. In 1936, he emphasized the importance of acknowledging and validating the other person's feelings before presenting an alternative perspective. While the feel, felt, found method is often used in conversations with others, it can also be a valuable tool for self-reflection and internal communication.

Three Steps:
1. **Feel:** Start by acknowledging your emotions. For example, you might say to yourself, "I feel overwhelmed right now."
2. **Felt:** Think about a time in the past when you felt the same way. Recall how you handled the situation and what you learned from it.
3. **Found:** Based on your past experiences, consider what actions helped you navigate similar feelings before. Try to apply those lessons to the current situation.

For example, someone might say to themselves, "I understand how I feel about this situation. I've felt this way before. I have found that there are other options I can explore." This method allows for acknowledging emotions from similar experiences and proposing alternative solutions.

Benefits:
- **Increased Self-Awareness:** Acknowledging your feelings and reflecting on similar experiences helps you better understand yourself.
- **Improved Problem-Solving Skills:** Finding a solution based on past experiences can help you develop helpful problem-solving skills and cope with challenging situations.

- **Enhanced Emotional Intelligence:** Empathy and self-reflection can enhance your emotional intelligence, allowing you to navigate relationships and communication more effectively.

Acknowledging your feelings, recognizing similar experiences, and discovering positive outcomes reduce feelings of hopelessness. Incorporating this method into your daily life can lead to a more fulfilling emotional journey.

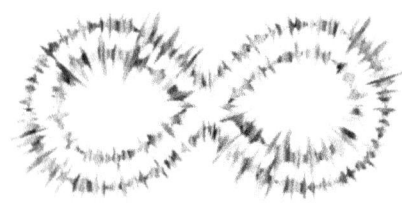

Embracing Healthy Discernment

Healthy discernment involves critically assessing information, evaluating choices, and determining the most appropriate action. For instance, when choosing a career, healthy discernment assists you with weighing the pros and cons of diverse options and selecting the one that aligns with your values and goals.

The ancient Greek philosopher Socrates believed in the importance of critical thinking and self-reflection in making decisions. He emphasized the need to question assumptions and seek the truth to make wise choices.

Imagine you're considering a job offer from a company with a questionable reputation. Healthy discernment would guide you to research the company, consider the potential consequences of working there, and make a thoughtful decision.

In personal relationships, healthy discernment can guide you in making mindful judgments that steer your life toward positive outcomes for yourself and others. It can also make you feel more in control and confident in your decisions.

One key aspect of healthy discernment is recognizing the difference between reliable information and misinformation. In today's digital age, where information is readily available online, it is essential to question the credibility of sources and fact-check before accepting any information as valid.

For instance, social media posts, unverified websites, and anonymous sources are often unreliable. Developing a healthy dose of evidence-based thinking can help individuals avoid falling for false or misleading claims.

Healthy discernment requires thinking ahead and weighing the potential outcomes of different choices. Reflecting on how our decisions may impact ourselves and those around us helps us make more responsible choices that align with our values and goals. This fosters a sense of accountability and maturity.

Seeking out diverse viewpoints and engaging in constructive dialogue allows individuals to gain a more comprehensive understanding of complex matters to make more informed decisions. It cultivates empathy and promotes mutual respect among people with differing opinions.

There is a delicate balance between trusting one's intuition while also relying on logic. Tuning into our inner wisdom and combining it with logical analysis helps us arrive at well-rounded decisions that consider our emotions and intellect.

Without healthy discernment, we risk making hasty decisions based on unreliable information, which can lead to adverse outcomes. Honing this skill empowers us to navigate challenges confidently, avoid pitfalls, and make choices that contribute to our overall well-being and success.

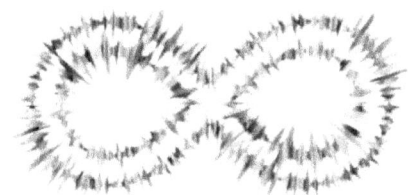

Remaining Objective

Remaining objective means staying neutral when evaluating a situation, topic, or problem. It means setting aside personal beliefs to be as fair or impartial as possible in your evaluation process. We can see things as they are rather than how we wish them to be.

Aristotle significantly contributed to various fields, including ethics, metaphysics, and logic. His work emphasized the importance of rational thinking. He believed one must set aside personal opinions and emotions to arrive at the truth.

Impact:
- **Making Informed Decisions:** When we are objective, we take the time to gather all the relevant information and consider different perspectives before making a decision. This helps us make choices based on facts rather than emotions.
- **Critical Thinking:** Remaining objective requires us to think critically, analyze information logically, and come to rational conclusions. It allows us to separate facts from opinions and avoid jumping to hasty conclusions.
- **Resolving Conflicts:** In conflicts or disagreements, being objective helps us see all sides of the issue and find a mutually beneficial solution that is fair to everyone involved. It promotes understanding and cooperation by reducing personal biases.
- **Creating Trust:** People are more likely to trust someone who is objective and fair in their judgments. Remaining neutral builds credibility and demonstrates a commitment to honesty.

Tips:
1. **Examine Your Biases:** Be aware of biases and prejudices that may influence your judgment. Acknowledging them helps you put them aside.
2. **Consider Different Perspectives:** Take the time to listen to different viewpoints and consider alternative opinions. This openness can help you better understand the issue at hand.

3. **Focus on Facts:** Base your decisions on evidence rather than assumptions or emotions. Separate what you know from what you believe.
4. **Stay Calm and Rational:** Regulate your emotions. Avoid letting anger, fear, or excitement cloud your judgment.

Examples:
- **Journalism:** Objective journalists strive to remain neutral when reporting the news by presenting facts accurately and without bias to ensure the public receives reliable information.
- **Scientific Research:** Objective scientists maintain neutrality in their research by following the scientific method, collecting data without bias, and drawing conclusions based on evidence rather than personal beliefs.
- **Legal System:** Judges and jurors are expected to remain objective during court proceedings while considering the evidence presented and applying the law impartially to ensure justice is served.

Staying objective empowers individuals to reveal their thoughts and feelings without fear of judgment. When we approach situations with an open mind and without bias, we create a safe space for genuine and honest communication.

Setting aside our opinions and listening attentively to others shows respect and empathy, which encourages vulnerability. Practicing objectivity promotes trust and understanding, paving the way for meaningful connections and emotional growth.

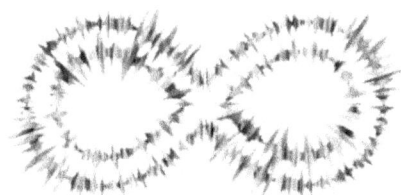

The Law of Averages

This statistical principle suggests that the outcomes of a series of similar events tend to even out over time. In the 16th century, Gerolamo Cardano recognized that over time, the outcomes of repeated events tend to stabilize around a certain average, leading to predictable results. This means that the more times an event occurs, the closer the results will get to their expected value.

When applied to communication with oneself, the law of averages can help individuals recognize that not every thought or feeling they have is a true reflection of reality. Just as in a series of coin flips where there will be both heads and tails, our thoughts and emotions can vary. This understanding puts us in control, allowing us to look at the big picture rather than getting stuck on individual moments.

Greed can sometimes lead people to misinterpret the law of averages, including in situations involving money or gambling. For example, someone might believe that if they keep playing a slot machine long enough, they will eventually win due to the law of averages. This misconception can drive individuals to make risky financial decisions to hit a big payout. They may fall prey to the allure of quick riches rather than understanding the actual probabilities at play.

Impact:
- **Recognizing Patterns:** Observing our thoughts and feelings over time helps us to identify patterns in our internal dialogue. This allows us to see that negative thoughts are worth investigating.
- **Balancing Perspectives:** When we catch ourselves engaging in negative self-talk, we can use the law of averages to balance it out. For every critical thought, we can challenge ourselves to produce a positive or neutral counterthought to bring the average back to a more balanced view.
- **Building Resilience:** Understanding the law of averages can also help build resilience in dealing with setbacks or failures. Instead of letting one negative experience dictate our self-perception, we can remember that it is just one data point in a series of events that will eventually balance out.

Tips:
1. **Journaling:** Keep a journal of your thoughts and emotions to provide a tangible record. Observe patterns and fluctuations in your internal dialogue. Review your entries at the end of each week to see how many positive, negative, or neutral thoughts you had.
2. **Challenge Negative Thoughts:** Once you recognize negative thinking patterns, challenge those thoughts with evidence. Ask yourself if those thoughts are based on facts or feelings. For instance, if you think, "I always mess up," consider times when you succeeded. Focus on the cases in which you performed well to shift the average of your self-talk toward positivity.
3. **Use Affirmations:** Repeat affirmations regularly to change the pattern of your thoughts over time. The law of averages suggests that the more you practice these affirmations, the more your mindset will shift.

   Examples of Affirmations:
   - "I am capable of achieving my goals."
   - "I learn from my mistakes."
   - "I am worthy of love and respect."
4. **Set Realistic Expectations:** Everyone makes mistakes and has setbacks. This shift in perspective helps remind you that it is normal to experience ups and downs. Create a list of goals, including the steps needed to achieve them. Aim for progress instead of expecting perfection. Celebrate small victories along the way.
5. **Surround Yourself with Positivity:** Engage with uplifting content, like motivational books or podcasts that inspire you. Surround yourself with supportive friends and family. Identify negative influences in your life and consider reducing your exposure to them.

The goal isn't to remove negativity altogether. It's to create a balance that fosters resilience and self-acceptance. As you practice these strategies, you will likely notice a positive change in your self-communication, improving confidence and overall well-being.

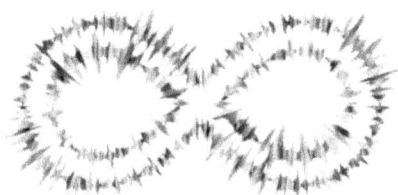

The Influence of Greed

When individuals succumb to the allure of greed, their focus shifts to material possessions, often at the cost of their relationships and well-being. It can distort internal dialogue if left unchecked, leading individuals to prioritize material wealth over personal growth.

When someone is consumed by greed, they may constantly seek validation through external sources such as money, status, or possessions. This constant craving for more can create a sense of emptiness and dissatisfaction, hindering their ability to engage in meaningful self-reflection.

As greed clouds their judgment, it can cause individuals to make decisions solely driven by personal gain rather than considering the moral implications of their actions. This can result in inner turmoil and a lack of authenticity as individuals struggle to reconcile their values with their desire for material wealth.

When greed takes center stage in interpersonal interactions, it can erode trust, empathy, and mutual respect among individuals. Communication driven by greed is often characterized by selfishness, manipulation, and a lack of genuine connection with others. It may prioritize desires at the expense of others, leading to strained relationships and conflicts.

Greed can hinder effective collaboration because individuals may be more inclined to compete rather than cooperate with others. This can create barriers to open communication, hinder productivity, and foster a hostile work environment.

Individuals or news outlets may prioritize sensationalizing a story to attract more viewers or followers, leading to misinformation being spread quickly through social media channels. This can result in confusion, panic, and delayed response to critical events, highlighting the importance of verifying information before sharing it.

Tips:
1. **Keep a Gratitude Journal:** Write down three things you are grateful for each day. This can shift your focus from what you want to what you already have.

2. **Focus on the Present:** Appreciate the moment you are in rather than constantly yearning for more. Mindfulness can help you enjoy the current experience without distractions.
3. **Identify What Matters:** Regularly reflect on your values, motivations, and actions to ensure they align with your goals beyond material gain.
4. **Set Healthy Boundaries:** Establish clear boundaries to prevent greed from dictating your actions by prioritizing mutual respect and empathy.
5. **Seek Balance:** Aim for a balanced approach to life that values personal growth and material well-being without letting greed overshadow other aspects of your life.
6. **Promote Generosity:** Practice acts of kindness and generosity towards others to foster a sense of community and cooperation.

Letting go of greed opens our hearts to understanding, compassion, and genuine communication. Our journey toward fulfillment is not about accumulating more. It's about recognizing the value of what we already have and the connections we build.

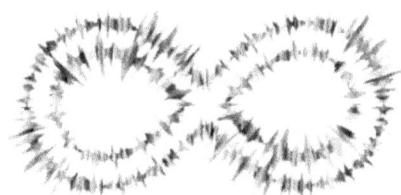

Urgent Communication

Urgency is the feeling of needing to act quickly. When it comes to communicating with oneself, urgency can lead to impulsive decisions. For example, imagine someone who has a big project due the next day. Feeling a sense of urgency to complete the project quickly may cause them to cut corners for completion, affecting the overall quality of the work.

Impact:
- In moments of stress or pressure, individuals may struggle to express their thoughts coherently, leading to misunderstandings. This can be problematic when communicating complex ideas or emotions to others.
- When someone is in a hurry or under pressure, they may come across as dismissive or curt in their conversations. This fast pace can create tension and hinder effective communication because the recipient may feel brushed off or ignored.
- During a disagreement, a sense of urgency to prove a point or win an argument can lead to escalated emotions and hostile communication. This heightened sense of urgency can prevent individuals from actively listening to each other or finding common ground.

Urgency often arises from a sense of pressure, fear of missing out, or the need to respond quickly to keep up with others. Recognizing the source of this urgency allows you to start addressing it effectively.

On the other hand, urgency can sometimes be beneficial in communication. In dire situations such as natural disasters or medical emergencies, a sense of urgency can prompt swift and decisive communication that saves lives. In these cases, urgency serves as a catalyst for clear and purposeful interaction.

During a drought emergency, urgent communication can quickly grab people's attention by highlighting the critical need to save water. Urgent messages about water scarcity can break through indifference and inspire individuals to take action to protect this treasured commodity for the benefit of the planet and all its inhabitants.

Tips:
1. **Pause and Reflect:** When you feel the urge to react immediately, take a step back. Give yourself a moment to reflect on your thoughts and emotions before communicating. This prudent time can help you respond more thoughtfully.
2. **Practice Mindfulness:** Engage in mindfulness techniques to help you stay concentrated during conversations. Practice deep breathing and grounding exercises to center yourself before communicating with others or making important decisions.
3. **Set Clear Communication Goals:** Before communicating, set clear goals for what you want to achieve. Whether it's expressing your feelings, sharing information, or resolving a conflict, having clarity on your communication goals can help you stay purposeful.

It is imperative to recognize when urgency drives our interactions and to take steps to mitigate its negative impact. Awareness of how urgency influences our communication style helps us slow down, clarify our thoughts, and express ourselves more effectively.

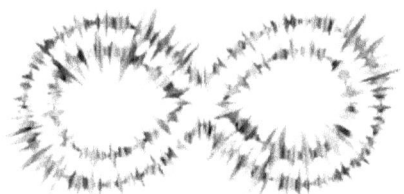

Impacting Indifference

Indifference can be described as a lack of interest or concern. When individuals become indifferent, they may struggle to express emotions, connect on a deeper level, and build strong relationships. This can be seen as insensitive, leading to misunderstandings, conflicts, and a sense of disconnect in personal and professional interactions.

Indifference towards oneself can manifest as self-neglect, low self-esteem, and a lack of self-awareness. When individuals are indifferent to their thoughts or emotions, they may struggle to identify and address their needs. This can result in inner turmoil, emptiness, and detachment from one's true self.

Impact:

- **Negative Self-Talk:** When we are indifferent to our feelings, it can lead to negative self-talk. For instance, if we fail a test and respond indifferently, we might think, "It doesn't matter. I'm not good at anything." This kind of thinking reinforces negative beliefs about ourselves.
- **Avoidance of Emotions:** If we do not acknowledge our feelings, we may push them aside instead of dealing with them. If we feel sad but choose to ignore it, our sadness does not go away. Instead, it can build up, affecting our mood or behavior later.
- **Lack of Motivation:** When we do not care about our goals or aspirations, we may find it challenging to take action. If someone feels indifferent about their performance, they may not make the necessary effort to complete their objectives. This lack of motivation can become a feedback loop that leads to poor outcomes.
- **Difficulty in Relationships:** Indifference can cause us to push people away. When we do not care about ourselves, it becomes challenging to care about others. If we are indifferent to our needs, we may struggle to empathize with the needs of friends and family. This can lead to feelings of alienation.

Tips:
1. **Identify Your Emotions:** Take time to reflect on how you feel throughout the day. Use an emotions chart to help recognize different feelings.
2. **Explore the Causes:** Consider what triggers your emotions. Understanding triggers can help you address them constructively.
3. **Meditation:** Spend a few minutes each day meditating. Focus on your breath. Observe your thoughts and feelings with compassion.
4. **Journaling:** Write down your experiences regularly. This helps you process emotions and understand your mental state better.
5. **Mindful Breathing:** When you feel indifferent, take a few deep breaths. This can help ground you and bring your focus back to the present.
6. **Challenge Negative Thoughts:** Ask yourself if your negative thoughts are true or if there is a more positive perspective.
7. **Affirmations:** Repeat positive statements about yourself, such as "I am capable of achieving my goals" or "I deserve to be happy."
8. **Smart Goals:** With clear objectives, we are more likely to care about our progress and outcomes. For example, instead of saying, "I want to be better at math," say, "I will complete three math practice problems every day for the next month."
9. **Visualize Your Goals:** Develop a vision board with images and words representing your goals. It serves as a daily reminder of what you want to achieve.
10. **Ask Questions:** Inquire how others perceive your communication style. Questions like, "Do I express my feelings clearly?" can lead to meaningful conversations.
11. **Active Listening:** Pay attention to how others communicate. Observe their techniques. Consider how you can incorporate their strategies into your self-communication.

Barriers caused by indifference can be broken down through intentional communication, cognitive reframing, and emotional engagement. Every improvement you make is a step toward a brighter future.

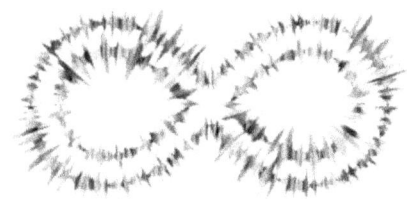

Cognitive Reframing

Cognitive reframing is a priceless psychological technique that helps individuals see situations from a different perspective. Its development can be attributed to the work of Albert Ellis in the 1950s and Aaron Beck in the 1970s, two prominent figures in the field of psychology.

Rather than fixating on negative thoughts or feelings, cognitive reframing encourages people to actively challenge and change their mindset, leading to a more productive outlook. Reframing their thoughts enables individuals to manage stress better, improve problem-solving skills, and enhance their overall emotional well-being.

One method of effective cognitive reframing involves three key steps. These steps consist of building up your thoughts and feelings, breaking them down to analyze them better, and building them up again with a beneficial perspective.

Dr. Nira Yuval-Davis is a prominent scholar in communication and social sciences. The "Build, Break, Build" method emerged from her research in the late 1990s and early 2000s. During this period, she was particularly interested in how societies construct identities and how these identities can be deconstructed or challenged.

This method is like constructing a mental puzzle. Start by putting the pieces together. Then, take a step back to see the bigger picture. Finally, rearrange the pieces to form a clearer image.

The Method:
1. **Build Up Your Thoughts and Feelings:** The first step in this cognitive reframing method is to build up your thoughts and feelings by expressing them in a productive manner. This can be done through journaling, drawing, or simply talking to yourself in a reflective manner. Putting your thoughts into words or images makes them easier to work with.

2. **Break Them Down:** Once you have documented your thoughts and feelings, it's time to break them down. Take a closer look at what you have written or drawn. Ask yourself questions like "Why do I feel this way?" or "What is the root cause of this thought?" Deconstructing your mental creations helps you to gain insights into your inner workings and identify patterns or triggers that influence your emotions.
3. **Build Them Up Again:** After analyzing your thoughts and feelings, it's time to build them up again with a fresh perspective. Use the insights you gained from breaking them down to reframe your thoughts constructively.

For example, if you identified a negative thought pattern, challenge it with a more balanced or empowering belief. Reconstructing your mental landscape cultivates a more compassionate and supportive inner dialogue.

Benefits:
- **Enhance Self-Understanding:** Actively exploring your thoughts and feelings develops a deeper understanding of your unique inner world.
- **Improve Emotional Intelligence:** Breaking down your emotions can help you identify triggers, manage stress, and respond to challenging situations with greater resilience.
- **Promote Self-Compassion:** Building up your thoughts with kindness and understanding can boost your self-esteem by fostering a more nurturing relationship with yourself.

Grab a journal or a sketchpad. Find a silent space where you can reflect without distractions. Then, start the process of cognitive reframing your thoughts and feelings. Effective communication with yourself is the foundation of personal growth that leads to healthier relationships with others.

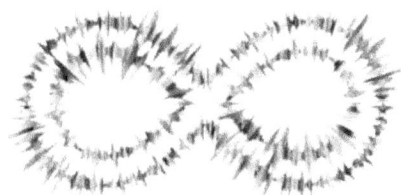

The ABCs of Constructive Communication

Feeling torn between choices or battling self-doubt can be challenging. One effective approach to resolving these internal conflicts is using a value-oriented solution. In 2018, I developed the ABCs of constructive communication, which focuses on alleviating internal conflict in three sentences.

Three Steps:
1. **Acknowledge:** The first step is to set a strong foundation with one statement of acknowledgment or appreciation. Every experience provides a personal truth that is worthy of acknowledgment, regardless of whether it is joy, sadness, anger, or excitement. This thinking builds a solid foundation for your communication structure.
2. **Belief:** The next step is to express one statement of your belief or concern about the related subject. This involves articulating your values, opinions, and worries honestly. Expressing your thoughts can help you clarify your position and identify the best course of action.
3. **Constructive Solution:** The final step in this method is to create one statement focused on a solution that supports the belief or resolves the concern. Progress is a lifelong process that involves learning from both successes and failures. Productive reinforcement can motivate you to continue working towards your goals.

Reflecting on personal beliefs helps individuals clarify what truly matters to them. This self-awareness helps them find resolutions that align with their core values. Constructive solutions allow people to foster authentic peace by effectively resolving internal conflicts.

Example 1:
1. **Acknowledgment:** "I am feeling unhappy despite my accomplishments."

2. **Concern:** "I am worried that if I reduce my efforts, I will disappoint someone."
3. **Constructive Solution:** "I can talk to someone about how I feel. If I explain my situation, they may understand and support my need to adjust my commitments."

Example 2:
1. **Appreciation:** "I am glad I accomplished my objective."
2. **Belief:** "I worked hard to achieve my goal."
3. **Constructive Solution:** "I will continue doing my best to meet my needs."

Tips:
- **Awareness:** Take a moment to reflect on your experiences. Reflect on what went awry, identify areas for improvement, and create a plan to move forward. Recognize what truly matters to you and what you want to achieve in the short and long term.
- **Aspirations:** Create a list of your goals while recognizing your core values. Choose the most beneficial path consistent with your core principles, even if it is more challenging. Resolving conflicts in a value-oriented manner cultivates a strong sense of self-respect and authenticity.
- **Gratitude:** Acknowledge your thoughts and emotions with appreciation through journaling.
- **Confidence:** Utilize affirmations. For example, you can say to yourself, "I am capable of achieving my goals" or "I have the resilience to overcome any obstacles." Repeat these affirmations regularly to strengthen your belief in your abilities.
- **Meditate:** Find a quiet space to be alone with your thoughts. Center yourself by taking a few deep breaths.
- **Expression:** Verbalize your beliefs or concerns aloud. You can also write a note to yourself addressing the issues that are weighing on your mind. Expressing your innermost concerns empowers you to gain clarity on the situation at hand.
- **Celebrate:** When you experience success, take the time to celebrate your achievements and acknowledge your hard work.
- **Growth Mindset:** View failure or setbacks as learning opportunities. Approaching them with a growth mindset allows you to bounce back more resiliently.

Resolving conflicts within yourself requires a solution-oriented approach. Aligning your actions with your values assists you with making decisions that honor who you are.

Mismanaged Abilities

When communication abilities are mismanaged, individuals may experience difficulties processing information. This can cause a phenomenon known as over-analysis paralysis, which is a state of overthinking or excessive criticism that hinders effective self-expression and decision-making. It can manifest in various ways, such as second-guessing decisions or feeling overwhelmed by emotions.

Individuals who struggle to manage their abilities may constantly question their thoughts and actions in a negative manner. This apprehension can create a cycle of anxiety and self-doubt, making it challenging to trust one's judgment and intuition.

Instead of processing information efficiently, individuals may get stuck in a loop of repetitive speculation called rumination. This can cause them to feel overwhelmed or mentally exhausted.

Impact:
- **Increased Self-Doubt:** We often focus on our flaws or mistakes when we overthink. This can lead to a negative self-image. For instance, someone who overthinks their performance on a project may convince themselves they did poorly, even if they received positive feedback from a mentor. This negative self-talk can damage their confidence and motivation.
- **Difficulty Making Decisions:** Overthinking can cloud our judgment. We may struggle to move forward when we analyze every possible outcome and worry about making the wrong choice. For example, an individual might spend hours deciding which hobby to enjoy. Fearing they will make the wrong choice can lead to missed opportunities and frustration.
- **Increased Stress and Anxiety:** Constantly worrying about our thoughts and actions can create pressure that affects our mental well-being. This is especially true for people who may already feel stressed about work, academics, social situations, or family expectations.

- **Reduced Problem-Solving Ability:** Overthinking can limit our ability to solve problems effectively. When we are stuck in a loop of negative thoughts, we may overlook simple solutions or fail to see the bigger picture. For example, a student might become so focused on a single math problem that they miss the overall concepts needed to solve it, leading to a lack of progress in their studies.

Tips:
1. **Practice Mindfulness:**
   - **Deep Breathing:** Take a moment to close your eyes and take deep breaths. Inhale through your nose for a count of four, hold for four, and exhale through your mouth for a count of four. Repeat this several times to calm your mind.
   - **Body Scan:** Scan your body using your hands. Go from head to toe while focusing on different parts of your body. Notice any tension or discomfort and consciously relax those areas.
   - **Observation:** Choose something in your environment. Observe it closely. Notice its color, shape, and texture. This practice can help ground you in the present moment.
2. **Challenge Negative Thoughts:**
   - **Identify Negative Thoughts:** Write down any negative thoughts you notice in your self-talk. This can help you see patterns in your thinking.
   - **Ask Questions:** For each negative thought, ask yourself questions like "Is this thought true?" or "What evidence do I have to support or contradict this thought?" This can help you evaluate the validity of your thoughts.
   - **Replace with Positive Affirmations:** Once you identify negative thoughts and challenge them, replace them with positive affirmations. For example, if you think, "I always mess up," replace it with "I am capable of learning from my mistakes."
3. **Set Time Limits for Decision-Making:**
   - **Choose a Time Frame:** Decide how much time you will spend thinking about a specific decision. For example, you might allow yourself ten minutes to decide what to eat for dinner.
   - **Make a Decision:** After your time is up, make a decision based on the information you have. Trust your instincts and move forward.
   - **Reflect:** After making the decision, take a moment to reflect on the outcome. Did it work out? How did you feel about your choice? This reflection can help you improve your decision-making skills over time.

4. **Journaling:**
   - **Daily Entries:** Set aside time to write about your thoughts and feelings each day. This can help you process your emotions and clarify your thoughts.
   - **Gratitude Journal:** Write down three things you appreciate each day. Focus on positive aspects of your life to alter your mindset and reduce negative thinking.
   - **Problem-Solving Journal:** If you are overthinking a specific problem, write it down and brainstorm possible solutions. This can help you feel more in control and lessen anxiety.
5. **Seek Support:**
   - **Join a Support Group:** Consider joining a group where you can share experiences with others who understand what you are going through. This can create a sense of community and support.
   - **Professional Help:** Mental health providers can offer support tailored to your needs.

Improving self-communication is a journey. It's okay to take it one step at a time. Addressing mismanaged abilities is imperative to maintaining a healthy internal dialogue, leading to a sense of control and confidence.

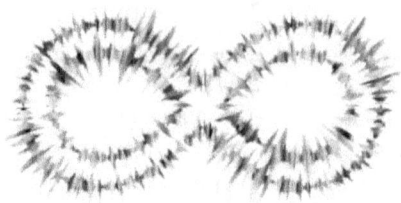

Practicing Mental Health

One of the extraordinary figures in the development of the concept of mental health is Hippocrates. He is an ancient Greek medical practitioner often called the "Father of Medicine." He believed that mental disorders were caused by an imbalance of the four biofluids, including blood, phlegm, black bile, and yellow bile.

According to Hippocrates, maintaining a balance among these fluids was essential for physical and mental health. His holistic approach to health emphasized the importance of diet, exercise, and a harmonious lifestyle.

In the 20th and 21st centuries, the theory of mental health has continued to evolve, with a greater focus on destigmatization, early intervention, and holistic approaches to mental well-being. Mental health practitioners are vital in helping individuals navigate through their internal and external behaviors.

While seeking support from these professionals can be beneficial, it is common for people to feel fearful or hesitant about reaching out for help. This fear can stem from several factors, including stigma, misconceptions, and past experiences.

Stigma and Misconceptions:
- One of the primary reasons why individuals may be afraid of mental health practitioners is the stigma attached to mental health issues. Unfortunately, society has not always been accepting or understanding of mental health challenges. This societal stigma can lead individuals to internalize negative beliefs about seeking help from a mental health professional. The fear of being labeled as "crazy" or "weak" by others can prevent individuals from seeking the support they need.

- Misconceptions about mental health practitioners can also contribute to fear. Some individuals may hold beliefs that mental health professionals are only for those with severe mental illnesses or that they will be judged for their thoughts and feelings. These misconceptions can create unnecessary barriers to seeking help and perpetuate the fear of judgment.

Fear of Being Judged:
- Another common reason individuals may perceive mental health practitioners as judgmental is the fear of being evaluated or criticized for their thoughts and behaviors. In seeking therapy or counseling, individuals may worry that the practitioner will view them negatively or make assumptions about their character based on the information shared.
- This fear of judgment can be influenced by past experiences of feeling misunderstood or criticized by authority figures. Damaging encounters with parents or other authority figures can lead individuals to anticipate a similar judgmental attitude from mental health professionals. As a result, individuals may hesitate to open up honestly during therapy sessions, fearing the consequences of being perceived negatively.

Effective Communication and Building Trust:
- To address these fears and misconceptions, mental health practitioners emphasize the importance of effective communication and building trust with their clients. Establishing a safe and compassionate space where individuals feel heard and validated is essential in overcoming the fear of seeking help.
- It is necessary for mental health providers to demonstrate empathy, understanding, and respect for their clients' experiences. Fostering a supportive and collaborative therapeutic relationship enables practitioners to help individuals feel more comfortable discussing their concerns and working towards positive outcomes.

Anxiety is a prevalent mental health condition that can cause overwhelming feelings of fear and uncertainty. When individuals experience anxiety, they may have intense moments of panic, rapid heartbeat, and difficulty breathing. Mental health professionals are critical in helping individuals manage these conditions by providing coping strategies.

Talking to a mental health professional doesn't mean there's something wrong with you. It means you're taking proactive steps to improve your mental well-being.

Online therapy provides a convenient platform for individuals to access mental health support from licensed therapists through online sessions. This innovative approach allows people to seek counseling from the comfort of their homes by eliminating barriers such as transportation or scheduling conflicts. Online therapy offers a range of options, including cognitive-behavioral therapy and mindfulness practices, tailored to meet the needs of each individual.

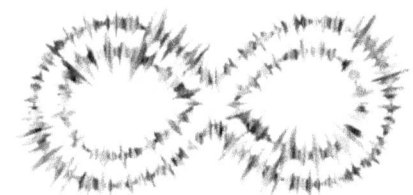

The Control Factor

There are things we can control and things we cannot. Differentiating between the two can help us navigate challenges and make informed decisions. Epictetus contributed ideas of control in the 1st and 2nd centuries C.E. Modern psychologists and philosophers have further explored and developed the concept of control.

What We Can Control:
- **Our Attitude:** While we may not always choose our circumstances, how we respond to them is within our control. Maintaining a positive attitude can substantially impact how we perceive and handle situations.
- **Our Effort:** Whether we put in extra study hours for a test or practice a new skill, our effort directly influences the outcomes we achieve. Giving our best effort increases our chances of success.
- **Our Reactions:** How we react to events and people around us is a choice we make. Develop healthy coping tools, such as deep breathing, mindfulness, or seeking social support. Emotional regulation skills can help us navigate challenging situations effectively.
- **Our Choices:** Every day, we face numerous choices, such as what to eat, how to spend our time, how to interact with others, and more. These choices shape the path that our lives take. Making informed decisions leads to positive outcomes.

What is Out of Our Control:
- **Others' Actions:** While we can influence and guide others, we cannot control their actions. Each individual is responsible for their behavior. Recognize that we cannot force others to act in a certain way.
- **Natural Events:** Natural disasters, weather patterns, and other natural events are beyond human control. While we can take precautions and adapt to these events, we cannot prevent them from occurring.

- **The Past:** While we can learn from previous experiences and use them to inform our decisions, we cannot change the past. Even if we could influence the past, we would potentially change our present reality, causing who we are and what we know to no longer exist.
- **Others' Opinions:** Just as we cannot control others' actions, we also cannot control their opinions of us. Each person has perspectives and beliefs that may not always align with ours. Be true to yourself rather than seeking validation from others.

Understanding what we can control and what is out of our control is pertinent for maintaining a sense of balance and well-being. Focus your energy on things within your control to increase your resilience and determination. Accepting things beyond your control can help you develop patience, humility, and a deeper appreciation for the world's complexities.

While we may not have control over every aspect of our lives, we have the power to influence our attitudes, actions, and decisions. Embracing this understanding encourages us to strive for personal growth and a greater sense of agency.

Embracing Limits

Have you ever felt frustrated when you couldn't do something perfectly? Think about when you tried something new and struggled to get the hang of it. It's completely normal to feel this way. Embracing the limitations of our capabilities is beneficial.

Understanding Our Limits:
- Our limitations are the boundaries or restrictions on what we can do. They can be physical, mental, or emotional. For example, you might have a physical limitation if you can't run extremely fast, a mental limitation if you struggle with math, or an emotional limitation if you get anxious in social situations.
- Keep in mind that everyone has limitations. Even the most talented and successful people face challenges and have things they can't do well. This universality of limitations is comforting because it means we are not alone in our struggles. The key is recognizing and accepting our limitations rather than letting them hold us back.

The Power of Acceptance:
- Embracing our limitations means accepting them for what they are and not letting them define us. Instead of seeing our limits as weaknesses, we can view them as opportunities for learning. When we acknowledge our limitations, we can work on improving ourselves to become the best version of who we are.
- If we never faced challenges or had things we couldn't do, how would we ever grow? Embracing our limitations allows us to develop resilience, creativity, and perseverance. It teaches us valuable lessons about patience, determination, and compassion.
- When we embrace our limitations, we open ourselves up to new possibilities. Instead of feeling defeated when you can't do something, believe that your abilities and wisdom can be developed through hard work and dedication.

Tips:
1. Understand your strengths and weaknesses.

2. View challenges as opportunities for improvement rather than threats to your self-worth.
3. Instead of giving up, ask for help.
4. Practice regularly.
5. Get out of your comfort zone by trying something new.
6. Find resources like online tutorials or books to support your learning.
7. Focus on progress rather than perfection to build confidence for skills that will serve you well in the future.
8. Break the topic into smaller, more feasible parts and tackle them one at a time.
9. Celebrate your progress toward a goal, no matter how small it may seem.

Success is not always about reaching the finish line first. It's about the journey and growth we experience along the way. Acknowledging our limits helps us set realistic goals, make better decisions, and focus on areas where we excel.

Accountability

Accountability involves taking ownership of our actions. We have a level of accountability in every situation we find ourselves in, even when we may not like the circumstances we are facing. During the Age of Enlightenment in the 17th and 18th centuries, philosophers began to explore the idea of individual responsibility in a systematic manner. This means that we are willing to acknowledge our role in creating a specific outcome regardless of whether it is favorable or unfavorable.

For example, imagine a scenario where a group of friends is working on a project together. Each group member has a specific task to complete, but one of them consistently fails to deliver on their responsibilities.

Failing to hold themselves accountable for their role hinders the group's progress and potentially jeopardizes the project's success. This scenario highlights how personal accountability is essential for teamwork and achieving common goals.

It is easy to embrace accountability when things are going well while we are experiencing success. However, true accountability is demonstrated when faced with adversity or challenging situations. Even when we may feel wronged or unfairly treated, we still have a responsibility to take ownership of our reactions.

Consider a situation where an individual receives poor feedback on a project they believe was unfairly evaluated. They may feel frustrated and tempted to blame the person providing input for the information received. Actual accountability would consist of reflecting on their preparation for the project, seeking clarification on the performance criteria, and taking steps to improve their achievement in the future.

Accountability empowers us to make positive changes in our lives and relationships. When we accept responsibility for our actions, we demonstrate integrity, resilience, and a willingness to learn. We also show respect for ourselves and others, which fosters trust and cooperation in our interactions.

Ryan Potter

When we are held accountable by setting goals with a friend or family member, we are more likely to stick to our healthy habits. Knowing that someone else is counting on us motivates us to stay committed to self-care. Being accountable to others can improve our health and encourage those around us to prioritize their well-being.

Maintaining healthy habits is crucial for our overall well-being. Taking care of our bodies is essential, whether exercising regularly, eating nutritious foods, or getting enough sleep. However, we may sometimes struggle to prioritize self-care during our busy lives.

Holding ourselves accountable allows us to learn from our experiences and make better choices in the future. Recognizing our accountability in every situation, even when faced with challenges or disagreements, empowers us to take control of our lives.

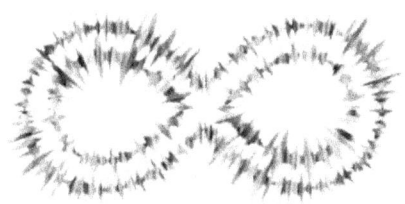

Mastering Inner Dialogue Skills

Mastering inner dialogue skills allows us to harness the ability to control our internal conversations effectively. Understanding that voice inside our head is indispensable because it can influence our emotions, decisions, and overall well-being.

When we master our inner dialogue skills, we can approach challenges with a growth mindset. Instead of letting self-doubt hold us back, we can embrace new opportunities. Developing strong inner dialogue skills enables us to control our thoughts better, leading to improved confidence and mental health.

Impact:
- **Building Resilience:** Challenges and setbacks are a natural part of life, but how we respond to them can make all the difference. Developing a resilient inner dialogue can reframe setbacks as opportunities for growth. This shift in perspective empowers us to bounce back with more determination than before.
- **Enhancing Self-Awareness:** We can intimately understand our emotions, beliefs, and behaviors. Engaging in reflective self-talk helps us pinpoint patterns of thinking that may be holding us back so that we can make conscious efforts to change them. This enlightenment enables us to align with our true selves.
- **Improving Relationships:** Mastering inner dialogue skills cultivates empathy, patience, and understanding in our interactions with friends, family, and peers. Positive self-talk can improve communication, conflict resolution, and overall relationship satisfaction.

Crucial inner dialogue skills:
1. **Embracing Positive Self-Talk:** Use constructive language when speaking to yourself. Instead of focusing on limitations and failures, recognize your strengths and potential. Adopting this mindset boosts confidence, resilience, and motivation.

2. **Practicing Self-Compassion:** Nurture yourself with warmth and understanding. Instead of being self-critical, offer yourself the same kindness you would give to a close friend who needs support while facing a challenge. This aspect provides emotional strength and a sense of inner peace.
3. **Cultivating Mindfulness and Awareness:** Be fully present in the moment. Tune into your thoughts and feelings. Pay attention to the content and tone of your self-talk. Identify recurring negative beliefs or thought patterns.
4. **Challenging Negativity:** Our thoughts and beliefs often hinder our growth and well-being. Question and reframe these destructive thoughts to make a significant change. Examine all the facts that counter this thinking. It can transform your outlook on life.
   - Instead of saying, "I can't do this," alter it with "I can learn how to do this with practice."
   - Modify "I'm not good enough" with "I am capable and deserving of success."
5. **Setting Realistic Goals and Intentions:** Align your thoughts and beliefs with achievable objectives. Set specific, measurable, attainable, realistic, and time-bound goals to motivate yourself to take action. Celebrate your progress along the way.

When our inner dialogue is focused on smart goal setting, we can overcome procrastination, self-doubt, and indecision. This will lead to greater productivity and fulfillment.

This ongoing process requires practice and patience. Taking the necessary time to make the effort will lead to a more purposeful life. Strive to make your inner dialogue empowering, uplifting, and supportive daily.

There's no time like today to start mastering your self-love and effective communication skills. How we talk to ourselves matters, so let's strive to be our best cheerleaders! If not now, when? Start today.

Encourage others to learn from this material and allow universal love to spread. Take action and leave a review on the site from which you purchased this book.

More To Come…

About The Author

Ryan Potter

    Hi, I'm Ryan Potter, the mind behind Body Smirks and the Self-Love Matters series. My journey began in 2010 when I graduated from the University of Houston. I received a bachelor's degree in Business Administration Marketing. I also earned certificates as an advanced sales professional and in corporate entrepreneurship. During my academic years, I was recognized with multiple awards for operations, creativity, and innovation, as well as being on the dean's list and at the top of my class.

    As the sole proprietor of Body Smirks since 2015, I bring a wealth of expertise to the table. I'm a licensed massage therapist, licensed massage instructor, certified reiki master, and certified in cognitive behavioral therapy. I offer services for massage, reiki, reflexology, gua sha scraping, facials, guided meditation, tarot card readings, and consultations for business and life coaching.

My commitment to helping people achieve long-term results in self-love matters is unwavering. The countless clients who have experienced transformation under my guidance are a testament to this. Their heartfelt testimonials shared on platforms like Google, Facebook, and MassageBook speak volumes about the value of my services.

Whether you are looking to improve your communication skills, enhance your self-care practices, or overcome mismanaged abilities, let this series for self-love matters be the guiding light that illuminates your path to personal growth, well-being, and happiness so that you can experience the new you!

www.ingramcontent.com/pod-product-compliance
Lightning Source LLC
Chambersburg PA
CBHW050522100526
44581CB00002B/82

www.ingramcontent.com/pod-product-compliance
Lightning Source LLC
Chambersburg PA
CBHW050522100526
44581CB00002B/82